Sea Kayaking
Florida
& the Georgia Sea Islands

OTHER TITLES AVAILABLE FROM OUT THERE PRESS

Sea Kayaking the Carolinas

Guides to Backcountry Travel & Adventure
North Carolina
South Carolina
Virginia
West Virginia
Tennessee (6/98)
Arkansas (9/98)

Sea Kayaking
Florida
& the Georgia Sea Islands

James Bannon

Out There Press
Asheville, North Carolina

Sea Kayaking Florida & the Georgia Sea Islands

© 1998 James Bannon

Out There Press
P.O. Box 1173
Asheville, NC 28802
out_there@earthlink.net

Maps drawn by James Bannon

Library of Congress Catalog Card Number: 98–65065
ISBN: 0–9648584–5–2

The author and publisher have made every effort to ensure the accuracy of the information contained in this book. Nevertheless, they can not be held liable for any loss, damage, injury, or inconvenience sustained by any person using this book. Readers should keep in mind that by its very nature sea kayaking contains elements of risk and danger. In other words, you're on your own out there. Be careful.

Cover photograph and design: James Bannon

Manufactured in the United States

10 9 8 7 6 5 4 3 2 1

For my Mother

Table of Contents

Map Symbols

Boat ramp

Camping Area

Daytrip

Weekender/Expedition

Visitor Center/Park Office

Other Building

Lighthouse

Town

Interstate

US Highway

State Highway

Secondary Road

Coral Reef

Abbreviations

4WD	Four Wheel Drive
E	east
ERR	Estuarine Research Reserve
ICW	Intracoastal Waterway
L	left
MM	mile marker
N	north
NPS	National Park Service
NS	National Seashore
NWR	National Wildlife Refuge
R	right
S	south
SP	State Park
SRA	State Recreation Area
W	west

Introduction

Trace the Southeast's coastline from Savannah, Georgia down past Miami to the tip of Florida and back up along the Gulf of Mexico to Pensacola and you've covered approximately 1,200 miles of mainland shoreline. Add in the hundreds of miles of barrier island coast and the perimeters of the hundreds of mangrove and coral keys in southern Florida, and the total is at least twice that. Then factor in a mild climate, just about perfect for outdoor activities at any time of year. Add to that an incredible diversity of flora and fauna, greater than in any other region of North America. The result is a subtropical paradise that seems to have been created with kayak touring in mind.

Although southern Florida has seen some of the most explosive development in the nation in the past half-century, and coastal Georgia continues to draw ever-growing numbers of tourists and residents, this region still boasts the largest wilderness areas east of the Mississippi River. The Everglades National Park alone encompasses 1.5 million acres in the southwest corner of Florida. And more than half of the Sea Islands that line Georgia's coast are protected as wildlife refuges, state preserves, or national seashore. Hundreds of square miles of the Florida Keys have been set aside as a wilderness. And the Gulf Coast remains wonderfully undeveloped between the beach resorts of the western panhandle and the Tampa/St. Petersburg metroplex.

These wilderness areas provide protection for the subtropical habitats that harbor more species of wildlife than anywhere else in the continental United States. There are tropical forests that reach their northern limits on the Florida Keys and are home to such exotic species as lignumvitae, black ironwood, gumbo-limbo, and Jamaica dogwood. There's the vast, golden prairie of the Everglades, the only ecosystem of its kind in the world and a refuge for the Florida panther, North America's most endangered mammal. Further north are barrier islands that grow forests of live oak so lush that the sun barely penetrates through the canopy. And salt marshes where herons, egrets, ibises, and dozens of other avian species stalk their prey. Alligators prowl the fresh-water rivers and brackish marshes of the region, including the Okefenokee Swamp, where there are more than 10,000 of the ancient reptiles. In the coastal waters are manatees and porpoises among the mammals, and tarpon, permit, mackerel, snook, bluefish, dolphin, pompano, and marlin to list just a few of the fish species. In Florida alone there are more than 450 different bird species, including the roseate spoonbill, sandhill crane, white-crowned pigeon, snail kite, bald eagle, and piping plover. In the underwater realm is the only living coral reef in the United States. Kayakers can don snorkeling gear and explore the vibrant corals and the brilliantly colored tropical fish they shelter and support.

In addition to the natural areas, the rich history and cultural heritage of Florida and Georgia can be experienced at some of their waterfront cities, towns, and fishing villages. Places like St. Augustine, the oldest city in the United States; or Key West, with a history as colorful and offbeat as any other place on the continent; or Cedar Key, where you can paddle all day from one deserted island to another, and then pull up at a waterfront restaurant for the catch of the day.

Whether you want to paddle in the wake of the Spanish, French, and British who all at one time settled this part of the Southeast, or disappear into a maze of mangrove islands or on to a deserted barrier island, the coastal regions of Florida and Georgia offer abundant opportunities.

Climate

The coastal regions of Georgia and Florida fall within the subtropical climate zone. The region's mild climate makes paddling here a year-round activity, and offers just enough variety to ensure that ideal conditions can almost always be found somewhere in the area covered by this book. The greatest variation in temperature is during winter, when there is a considerable difference between southern Florida and Georgia. Summers in both Georgia and Florida are hot and humid, with daytime temperatures often exceeding 90°. Ocean and Gulf breezes help to moderate the temperature somewhat along the coast, particularly compared to the inland, where the heat can be unrelenting and oppressive.

Winters, on the other hand, vary considerably across the 500-mile range between Savannah and Miami. Paddlers will find winters chilly along the Georgia coast and Florida Panhandle, with daytime temperatures often not getting above the 50s, and nighttime lows dropping to near freezing. Water temperatures drop accordingly, and kayakers will need to be prepared with layers of clothing that provide insulation and waterproofness.

Weather

As a region, the Southeast is characterized by some of the most pleasant weather in North America, punctuated every now and then by storms of unsurpassed fury and intensity. In the grand scheme of things, it seems like a reasonable trade-off: 300 days each year of sunny weather in exchange for the possibility that for a day or two 125 mph winds will lash the land and chase every living thing on it underground. The season for hurricanes and tropical storms runs from early summer through late fall. Some years pass without a single intense storm; in others, they seem to line up across the Caribbean every month or so. Summer is also the season for afternoon thunderstorms. While these storms may seem to follow a predictable pattern, they can arise suddenly, and at any time. Paddlers going out for more than a day should consider a weather radio essential equipment, particularly for long trips during hurricane season.

For coastal kayakers, air and water temperature, and wind speed and direction, are all major concerns. Each of these factors will have an impact on any kayaking trip. Before setting out, you should check both the current conditions and forecast for the location of your trip. Weather charts showing air temperature, water temperature, wind speed, and prevailing wind direction are located at the start of each of the three main sections in this book.

Tides & Current

In addition to the weather, the other factors with the greatest impact on paddling conditions are the lunar tides and prevailing currents.

All but one of the paddling routes covered in this book are on bodies of water affected by tides. Tidal ranges along the coastline of Georgia and Florida vary from 1 foot to more than 7 feet. The tides are highest along the Georgia coast, where it is just about essential to plan a trip to coincide with the tides; paddling away from the coast on an ebb tide, and back in on a flood tide.

Keep in mind too that as tides ebb and flood they vary in intensity. The rule of twelfths is a useful mnemonic: during the first hour of a tide, one-twelfth of the water is displaced, during the second hour, two-twelfths, during the third hour, three twelfths, during the fourth hour, three-twelfths, during the fifth hour, two-twelfths, and during the sixth hour, one-twelfth. In other words, on a six foot tide, the water will rise or fall a half foot in the first hour (one-twelfth of six), a foot in the second hour, a foot and a half in the third hour, etc. Paddling with a strong tide can shorten your trip or allow you to cover greater distances, while paddling against a strong tide can result in a lot of work and little progress. It's not unusual in Georgia for the combination of wind and tide to make it impossible to make *any* progress paddling against the tide.

One exception to seeking to take advantage of a tide when it's at its strongest is when crossing a channel or inlet. These are easiest to negotiate during a slack tide, i.e. when the tide is changing directions. At those times the least amount of water is moving and therefore the current is slowest. Tide tables that give the times for local high and low tides (and sometimes the range) are available for free at most marine and fishing supply stores on the coast.

In addition to currents caused by the lunar tide cycle, several other types of currents are encountered on the coast of Georgia and Florida. River currents move from inland bodies of fresh water to the ocean. Due to the flat topography of the coastal plain, these currents are generally mild, though large rivers, such as the Altamaha, flow with a powerful force. Currents at a river's delta, or mouth, can be strong, unstable, and unpredictable, since a steady flow of river water is continually crashing into a vast body of water with a tidal flow of its own. Only skilled kayakers should attempt to navigate these waters. Strong ocean currents, running both parallel and perpendicular to shore, are another factor to keep in mind.

When to Go

At any time of year, sea kayakers can find just about ideal conditions somewhere in the area covered by this book. Almost all of the coastal areas in Georgia and Florida are popular tourist destinations, with definite seasonal cycles. In Georgia and the Florida panhandle, the peak season is summer. In southern Florida, intense heat, seasonal rains, and mosquitoes keep people away during the summer and fall, while vacationers flock there by the millions from December to April. Paddlers who follow the typical tourist patterns will be rewarded by the best weather and climate of the year, but will have to tolerate the inevitable crowds. And on the water, you'll have to share space with fishing boats, pleasure cruisers, jet-skis, and water-skiers. Since kayak touring is as much about exploring wild, remote regions and observing natural habitats as it is about having fun in the sun, shoulder seasons and off seasons can offer conditions that are as good as or better than at the peak tourist times. Certainly finding a campsite or a hotel room will be easier, and in most cases, cheaper.

Spring and fall are delightful in Georgia and the Florida Panhandle. The summertime crowds are absent from the major seaside resorts, but temperatures are still warm and the days still relatively long. And south Florida, which can be hot in spring and rainy in fall, also has periods of sunny, pleasant days. For solitude and wildlife observation, winter beats all the other seasons combined, at least north of Miami and Tampa/St. Petersburg. The number of visitors to the beaches dwindles from the thousands to the tens, with an opposite proportion of avian species. Both Georgia and Florida are located along the Atlantic Flyway, the major migratory route for birds in the East. Literally hundreds of species of waterfowl, song birds, raptors, and shore birds pass through each year or settle in for the winter. One species that isn't present during these months is the mosquito, so abundant in backcountry locales at other times of year.

In south Florida, on the other hand, winter is peak season. While the Everglades and Keys are most crowded during this time of year, the swarms of mosquitoes, frequent rainstorms, blistering sun, and oppressive heat are factors to keep in mind if you plan to visit from May to October. There are few wild places in the United States that can match a summer day in the Everglades for conditions that seem designed to torture humans.

Kayak Touring

For centuries, sea kayaks have provided travellers with a means of reaching otherwise inaccessible areas of wilderness. A kayak's natural stealth and shallow draft make it ideal for exploring sensitive coastal environments. Unlike motor boats, kayaks permit travel through wildlife habitats without disturbing or causing undue stress to the natural habitats or native species. And unlike backpacking, it permits you to carry the gear required for backcountry camping without having to shoulder the load yourself. With an average rate of travel of about 3 miles per hour, a kayak allows you to cover as many as 30 miles of travel in a day, though a more typical day's paddle will cover 10–20 miles. Rates of travel and distances covered will of course depend on a number of factors, including tides, currents, wind, paddling technique, and your personal level of endurance. All of the trips described in this book cover fewer than 20 miles per day.

What to Bring

What you bring with you on a particular paddling trip will depend on several factors: destination, length of trip, time of year, and weather. When preparing a packing list for a trip, include whatever you'll need for the worst conditions you're likely to encounter. While this may seem like a pessimistic way of thinking about an upcoming paddling trip, it will also help prevent you from being caught unprepared. A trip can quickly turn from a pleasant outing to a miserable nightmare if you arrive on a buggy island with no insect repellent, get caught in a rainstorm without shelter or rain gear, paddle beneath a scorching sun without adequate protection, or run out of water on the second day of a three-day expedition, to name just a few possible scenarios. Aside from the standard safety items that should be part of any trip, the most essential items for paddling in the Southeast are lots of water, sunblock, insect repellent, and a hat with a brim.

Items you should carry with you when kayaking have been arranged here in three groups: safety items, day-trip items, and camping-trip items. Items in the first two lists should be considered essentials (with the obvious exceptions, such as a camera). Items included under camping trips are in addition to those listed under day-trip items. The kayak supply stores listed in the appendix at the back of this book can provide you with supplies and offer suggestions. Many of the items are also available from general outdoor supply stores.

Safety Items

PFD (personal flotation device, required by law)
Spare paddle
Pump
Dry Bag
Change of clothes
Compass
Topo map or NOAA chart (or both)
First-aid kit
Flare
Weather radio
Tide table

Day-trip Items

Drinking water
Suntan lotion
Rain gear
Sunglasses
Trash bag
Flashlight
Paper towels
Camera
Fly rod & reel

Insect repellent
Hat with brim or visor
Long-sleeve shirt
Food
Pocket knife
Waterproof matches
Binoculars
Field guides
Tow Rope

Camping Items

Tent (w/ extra long stakes)
Sleeping bag
Stove
Utensils
Personal hygiene kit
Paddle float

Ground cloth
Sleeping pad
Cook set
Biodegradable soap
Lantern

Backcountry Camping

Many of the trips described in this book are multi-day journeys with at least one night spent camping in the wilds. These backcountry camping areas are often in pristine natural habitats that are fragile and very sensitive to human impact. Many are located in preserves designed to protect endangered or rare flora and fauna. All are part of the ever-decreasing pockets of wilderness left in the United States. In other words, people are only visitors. The same guidelines that apply to low-impact wilderness travel elsewhere are valid for kayak camping as well.

In general, you should strive to leave no evidence of your visit behind. This means choosing campsites that will have a minimum impact on sensitive areas; restoring campsites to a natural appearance; packing out all refuse; resisting the impulse to build fire rings; and using a camp stove for cooking, rather than an open fire. If you do build a fire, use only dead and downed wood.

Self-Rescue

The one safety technique that all paddlers should have before getting into a kayak is the ability to perform a wet exit. This is simply a means of exiting the boat in the event of a capsize. Of course, the ability to get back into the kayak is a useful skill as well. If you've never kayaked before, you should practice in a pool or sheltered body of water with a friend on hand to help before heading out on a trip.

A more advanced self-rescue technique is the Eskimo Roll. Simply put, the Eskimo Roll is a means of righting an overturned kayak without exiting the boat. It is an essential maneuver in white water kayaking, one that any proficient white-water paddler can manage with relative ease. While it is undoubtedly the quickest way to restore an overturned sea kayak to an upright position, it is not considered an essential skill. There are several reasons for this. First of all, sea kayakers usually ply much calmer waters than white-water kayakers, and instances of capsizing are the exception, rather than the norm. Second, if you do capsize, you won't have thousands of pounds of river current pushing you relentlessly forward. And third, performing an Eskimo Roll in a sea kayak, especially one loaded with camping gear, can be extremely difficult, if not impossible. Many sea kayaks have cockpits so roomy that they simply aren't designed to provide the leverage needed to execute an Eskimo Roll. Unless conditions are particularly severe, you should be able to exit the boat, turn it back upright, pump it out, and get back in. An Eskimo Roll, if you can perform one, will certainly shorten the procedure of righting yourself and the boat, but since danger isn't usually a factor, it isn't essential from a rescue point-of-view.

Using this Book

Sea Kayaking Florida & the Georgia Sea Islands is a where-to, as opposed to a how-to, guide to kayaking. While it does include some incidental information about technique and preparation, it was written with the assumption that those using it have received instruction in kayaking from some other source, be it a book, friends, or a course. If you've never kayaked before, you shouldn't use this guide as your sole introduction to the sport. Read other books or magazines on the subject; take a trip with friends who are experienced kayakers; or sign up for a course or guided trip. Outfitters that offer the latter are listed in the back of this book.

The book's layout is intended to help you choose a destination and then get you on the water with as little fuss as possible. Descriptions of trips are kept short. Rather than writing a lengthy narrative of my own experience paddling a particular route or area, I've simply provided the necessary information for you to assess an area and follow a chosen route. I've tried to include all the information that is most useful to kayakers planing a trip: location of put-ins and take-outs, potential hazards, tidal ranges, on-site sources of information, camping facilities and regulations, and the location of water and other facilities.

Each entry begins with a descriptive sketch that gives a general overview of an area. The focus here is on the aspects that make the area an appealing, and often unique, paddling destination, with an emphasis on natural habitats, wildlife, historical background, and opportunities for other outdoor activities. Following are shorter entries that provide specific information. In order, they are: information, maps, hazards, base camp, and trip descriptions. The specific information included under each of these headings is described below.

INFORMATION: This section includes the name, address, phone number, and internet address of a contact who can supply you with additional information about an area. In most cases, this is the administrative body that oversees the particular area. Often, there's an on-site office or headquarters where you can pick up maps (usually *not* NOAA charts or USGS topos, however), brochures, or check on local conditions. This is always a good idea before heading out, and often you'll be asked to leave an itinerary and check back in at the end of your trip. Also included here is the nearest location of facilities such as water, rest rooms, and pay phones.

MAPS: Along with a compass, a good map should be considered essential equipment for most of the trips described in this book.

The best maps for coastal kayaking are the NOAA charts used by all boaters and the USGS topographic maps familiar to backpackers and hikers. Which you use is largely a matter of personal preference and where you'll be paddling. The topo maps are best for reading landscapes, while the NOAA charts are particularly good for navigating shallows and tidal flats. For the topos, the 7.5-minute series is preferred because of its large scale. The NOAA charts come in various scales. The 1:40,000 and 1:80,000 charts are the most suitable for kayaking. These are available at most marine supply stores. The USGS topo maps are available at many outdoor supply stores or from the U.S. Geological Survey, Branch of Distribution, Box 25286, DCF, Denver, CO 80255.

The maps included in this book are for illustration purposes only. They are only meant to provide a visual aid to area descriptions and should not be used for navigation.

HAZARDS: This is perhaps the trickiest section in the book. While the large majority of kayaking trips are undertaken without incident, and I don't want to create a misleading sense of apprehension, I also don't want to encourage a false sense of security—or worse, of invulnerability. As with all types of outdoor travel and adventure, an element of risk is involved in sea kayaking. My aim is to help you be aware of that risk in order to minimize it. Under this section I've included only hazards that are particular to an individual area. This does not mean that they are the only hazards that will be encountered. Hazards common to the Florida and Georgia coast such as strong winds, rip tides, unpredictable currents, sudden storms, and hurricanes are not included under this section. This does not mean that they should be discounted. In using this section, always treat the list of hazards as incomplete. At the end of this section the average tidal range for the area is given.

BASE CAMP: Unfortunately, we don't all live next to pristine coastal areas. Except for short day-trips close to home, you'll need to find some place to settle down for the night. In keeping with the book's focus on backcountry travel, I've looked first for primitive campsites or campgrounds that can serve as a convenient base for day-trips or weekend trips into the backcountry. In some cases there are backcountry campsites designed to accommodate paddlers, or primitive backcountry camping is permitted at an area accessible either by boat or on foot, as at St. Joseph Peninsula State Park. More often, however, you'll find yourself based at a developed campground near the put-in or take-out. I've also included the town or city with hotels, motels, and B&Bs closest to each area. Just in case you would actually rather sleep on a bed than in a tent after a day out on the water.

PUT-IN: Directions are given from the nearest large town or highway. Many of the put-ins are developed boat ramps. Others are sandy landings or unimproved ramps designed for canoes and kayaks. All have parking, unless indicated otherwise.

TAKE-OUT: More often than not, the take-out is the same as the put-in. While round trips often require some retracing of your route, you at least won't have to use two cars or make arrangements for a vehicle shuttle. A couple of the trips are one-way and end at a location different from the put-in.

DAY TRIP: The description of each trip begins with a brief encapsulation that includes trip highlights, beginning and ending points, distance, and a difficulty rating. These last 2 items are described in separate sections below.

At least one day trip is included for each of the areas in this book. In all but a few cases, the trips range from 5 to 20 miles. Assuming an average paddling speed of 3 mph, this means a trip that ranges in length from just under 2 hours to more than 6, not counting rest stops or lunch breaks. Keep in mind that the routes described are suggestions only. In most cases, the recommended trips can be shortened or lengthened to suit personal preferences. At some of the larger areas, such as Everglades National Park, there are almost as many potential routes as there are paddlers.

TRIP DISTANCE: All distances are given in land miles, rather than nautical miles. The reasons for this are that everybody is familiar with land miles and they're used on the scales of all maps except nautical charts. To convert the distances to nautical miles, simply add 15 percent to the land mile distance (a nautical mile is 6,076 feet).

DIFFICULTY RATING: The difficulty rating is a subjective measure devised by the author of this book to provide readers an easy scale for evaluating trips. The scale runs from 1 to 5, with 1 being the easiest and 5 the most difficult. The numbers of the scale have no meaning outside of this book and do not relate to any other scale. You should also be aware that the scale only refers to conditions encountered in the areas covered by this book. In other words, a 5 refers to the most difficult conditions you will encounter paddling in Georgia or Florida, not the most difficult conditions you could encounter paddling elsewhere.

The criteria used in assigning these ratings are as follows: size of body of water, proximity to dry land or shallow water, strength of currents, prevailing wind conditions, ease of rescue, and volume of other boat traffic. In assessing a particular trip, the ratings can be read as follows:

1. Easy, suitable for novices. A good learning environment.
2. Easy to moderate, but requiring at least a measure of skill.
3. More difficult. May involve paddling on open water and negotiating hazards. Self-rescue required.
4. Difficult. Involves conditions that require considerable experience, such as crossing large bodies of open water.
5. Very difficult. The most demanding conditions encountered in Florida or Georgia. Obvious obstacles to self-rescue, such as very strong currents or remoteness.

These ratings apply to typical paddling conditions during warm weather with water temperatures above 65°. When conditions are less favorable or when the water temperature is below 65°, the difficulty rating would increase depending on the severity of the conditions.

WEEKENDER: The definition of a weekender is two day's paddling with a single overnight. Most of the information for this category is the same as for the daytrip. The major difference is that all weekenders involve some form of camping, usually in a primitive undeveloped area with few or no facilities. In addition to paddling skills, these trips require a knowledge of low-impact backcountry travel and wilderness survival. Many of the trips involve making camp on an empty beach or in a wilderness preserve miles from civilization. Overnighting in these remote locales requires additional preparation and care to ensure your own safety and to protect environments that are fragile and easily damaged.

EXPEDITION: Similar to a weekender, except longer. A small handful of the areas covered in this book are large enough to permit trips of three days or longer. These trips will appeal to experienced paddlers or to adventurous novices. For this reason, the trip descriptions have been left intentionally vague, with the thought that paddlers will want to choose their own routes and itineraries. Considerable advance planning is required, with contingencies for bad weather and other unforseen circumstances.

The Atlantic Coast

The Atlantic Coast Key Map

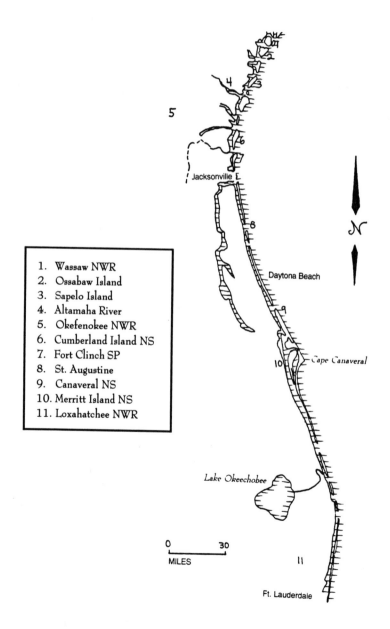

1. Wassaw NWR
2. Ossabaw Island
3. Sapelo Island
4. Altamaha River
5. Okefenokee NWR
6. Cumberland Island NS
7. Fort Clinch SP
8. St. Augustine
9. Canaveral NS
10. Merritt Island NS
11. Loxahatchee NWR

Jacksonville

Daytona Beach

Cape Canaveral

Lake Okeechobee

Ft. Lauderdale

0   30
MILES

Weather Readings at Savannah, GA

Month	Air Temp (High F°)	Water Temp F°	Wind Speed (mph)	Wind Direction
January	62°	51°	8.5	WNW
February	64°	52°	9.5	NE
March	69°	60°	9.5	WNW
April	76°	67°	9	SSE
May	83°	74°	8	SW
June	88°	80°	7.5	SW
July	89°	85°	7.5	SW
August	89°	85°	7	SW
September	85°	81°	7.5	NE
October	77°	72°	7.5	NNE
November	70°	64°	7.5	NNE
December	62°	54°	8	NE

Weather Readings at Cape Canaveral, FL

Month	Air Temp (High F°)	Water Temp F°	Wind Speed (mph)	Wind Direction
January	68°	61°	9	N
February	70°	59°	9.5	N
March	75°	65°	10	ESE
April	80°	71°	10	ESE
May	85°	77°	9	ESE
June	88°	80°	8	E
July	90°	80°	7.5	ESE
August	89°	80°	7	ESE
September	87°	82°	8	ENE
October	82°	77°	9	E
November	76°	71°	8.5	NW
December	70°	65°	8.5	NW

Wassaw National Wildlife Refuge

Wilmington River ◊ Wassaw Sound ◊ Atlantic Ocean

Less than half an hour from historic downtown Savannah, the Wassaw National Wildlife Refuge encompasses 10,070 acres of sandy beach, dune, maritime forest, and salt marsh. A pair of uninhabited, undeveloped islands, Wassaw Island and Little Wassaw Island, comprise the refuge and provide habitat for a variety of wildlife species. During winter migrations, the number of waterfowl, shore birds, and other avian species that visit the refuge brings the total number into the hundreds. Among these are pelicans, cormorants, egrets, herons, gulls, and the endangered bald eagle. On land, white-tailed deer forage in the uplands, loggerhead sea turtles come ashore to nest, and the poisonous diamondback rattlesnake is sometimes seen. More evident are the dolphins that paddlers often encounter swimming in the sheltered waters of the sound or the lower reaches of the Wilmington River.

The island is only accessible by boat, and most trips begin from just outside Skidaway Island State Park, located on the barrier island of the same name that's separated from the mainland by the Intracoastal Waterway. The park offers paddlers a convenient base from which to set out on explorations of Wassaw Island. Habitats on Skidaway Island are similar to those on Wassaw Island, with fresh and salt marshes, forests of pine, palmetto, and live oak, and shrub thickets. A short nature trail and observation towers permit exploration of the island on foot.

Wassaw Island is also open to exploration, and once you land on the island you'll at least want to spend some time wandering along the beach and checking out the dead trees that rise from the sand like ghostly skeletons. Although a large percentage of the island is marsh, the solid uplands on the island's Atlantic side are traversed by a series of primitive roads that are open to hikers. The roads cut through forests of slash pine, live oak, and cabbage palmetto. The woodlands provide protection and sustenance for most of the refuge's mammal and reptile species: white-tailed deer, raccoon, squirrel, and diamondback rattlesnake.

The 7-mile beach, deserted on most days, offers opportunities

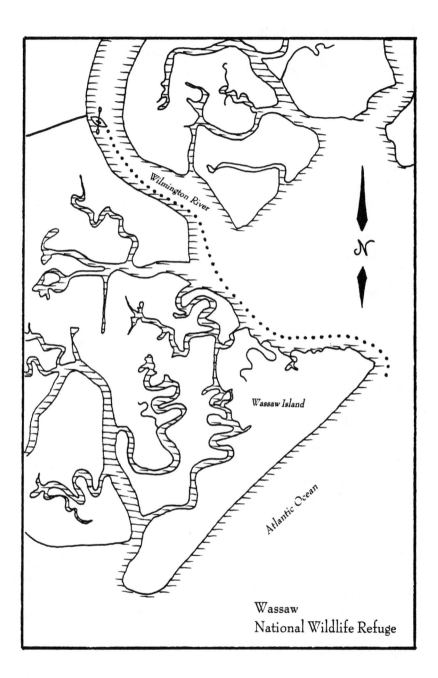

Wilmington River

N

Wassaw Island

Atlantic Ocean

Wassaw
National Wildlife Refuge

for swimming, sun-bathing, or fishing. The refuge is only open to visitors during daylight hours, and camping is not allowed. There are no facilities and no on-site source of information on Wassaw Island. Keep in mind that the tidal currents along the shore are very strong and that there's no one to come to your rescue if you get in trouble.

INFORMATION: Savannah Coastal Refuges, Parkway Business Center, Suite 10, 1000 Business Center Dr., Savannah, GA 31405; 912/652-4415; www.fws.gov/~4reao/nwrwsw.html. There's no visitor center or other development on the refuge. Use Skidaway Island State Park (912/598-2300) as a base. A $2 entrance fee is charged there.

MAPS: NOAA 11512; USGS Isle of Hope, Wassaw Sound.

HAZARDS: Swift tidal currents and tricky waters at the mouth of the river and where the sound meets the ocean are the main challenges to paddlers. Commercial fishing boats are often present in the sound. Tidal range: 7 feet.

BASE CAMP: The attractive car campground at Skidaway Island State Park makes an ideal base for day trips to Wassaw Island. Sites cost $14–17/night and the campground is open year round. Hotels, motels, and B&Bs are available in Savannah, less than 10 miles away. Contact the Savannah Visitors Bureau (800/444-2427) for listings.

PUT-IN: From I-95, take exit 16. Turn E onto GA-204 and go 10.5 miles to Montgomery Cross Rd. Turn R and go 1.3 miles to Waters Ave. Turn R and go 5.8 miles (at 5.3 miles turn L between the two churches to reach Skidaway Island SP) to McWhorter Dr. Turn L and go 2 miles to a fork. Bear R and go 1 mile to the end of the road and a primitive put-in. If the tide is in you can launch here; if it's out, portage about 100 yards to the R and launch from the UGA boat ramp.

An alternate put-in is on the Intracoastal Waterway on the

mainland side of the bridge to Skidaway Island, 1 mile before the state park entrance.

TAKE-OUT: Same as the put-in.

DAY TRIP: *Tidal Creek to Barrier Island. This 11-mile round-trip paddle takes you past the luxury homes of Skidaway Island to uninhabited Wassaw Island. Highlights are dolphins, a multitude of shore birds, and the long sandy beach of Wassaw Island. Difficulty Rating: 3.*

The strong tidal currents on this route make it almost essential that you time your trip to coincide with the ebb and flood tides. From the put-in, paddle past the UGA dock and down the Wilmington River. As you reach the river's mouth after almost 3 miles, swells begin to appear and open water conditions intensify. At the mouth of the river is Wassaw Sound, from which the island comes into view to the R and ahead. Paddle E toward the sandy point and the long strand of beach that stretches away from it. At 5.5 miles you reach the point—you can land here or at any point along the 7 miles of sandy beach. The breakers are usually insignificant here and surfing to shore shouldn't present much of a problem. When you're ready to return, follow the same route back to the put-in/take-out.

Ossabaw Island State Heritage Preserve
Red Bird Creek ◊ Ogeechee River ◊ Ossabaw Sound ◊ Atlantic Ocean

Ossabaw Island is one of the largest, and also one of the most remote and least visited, of Georgia's string of barrier islands. The only way to reach the island is by boat, and for kayakers, the paddle is a long one. And once you're on the island you won't find a visitor center to check in at, a campground to overnight at, or even a drinking fountain to top off your water bottle. In fact, there aren't any facilities or development on the island at all. Ossabaw Island is coastal Georgia at its wildest.

For those who are willing to make the arduous trip out from the base camp at Fort McAllister State Park, however, the rewards are ample. The 9.5-mile-long island occupies almost 12,000 acres of beach, dunes, shrub thicket, and live oak, palmetto, and pine woodlands. Another 13,000 acres of salt marsh sprawl westward from its back edge. This latter habitat is a vital breeding ground for literally hundreds of marine species that will either remain in the sound for their entire lives or leave it for the more perilous waters of the ocean once they have reached maturity. The abundance of marine life attracts a whole host of birds—great blue herons, great and snowy egrets, osprey, and dozens of others dive from the sky above or stalk the flats in search of their next meal. The island is on the Atlantic Flyway, which means that during fall and winter migrations the populations and diversity of bird species rise dramatically. Waterfowl such as mallards and teal, and sandpipers, warblers, thrushes, sanderlings, and plovers join the wading birds and shore birds that make the region their year round home.

Journeys to Ossabaw Island must first pass through a variety of different coastal environments before reaching their destination. Red Bird Creek is a narrow, tidal waterway that slides and bends through the vast golden prairie of the salt marsh. It empties out onto the Intracoastal Waterway, which can be busy with sailboats, fishing boats, and luxurious yachts. The Ogeechee River, which drains into Ossabaw Sound and the Atlantic Ocean, is one of the major waterways in the region.

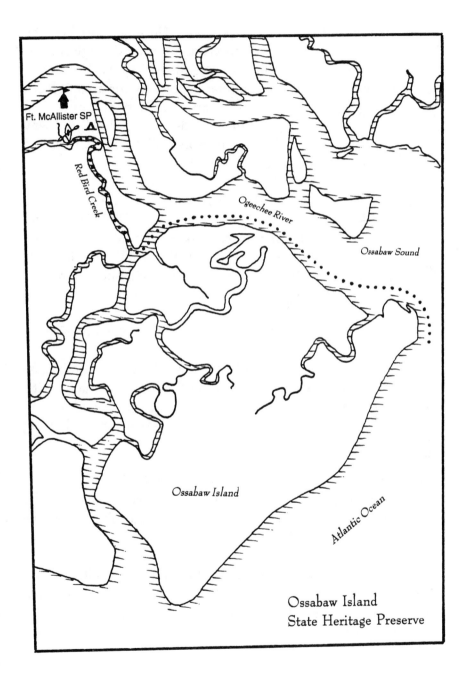

Ft. McAllister SP

Red Bird Creek

Ogeechee River

Ossabaw Sound

Ossabaw Island

Atlantic Ocean

Ossabaw Island
State Heritage Preserve

Ossabaw Island is managed as a State Heritage Preserve, the first in Georgia. It is only open to visitors during daylight hours, so only day trips are possible. Fort McAllister State Park is a ideal base if you want to spend several days exploring the area. It has a short hiking trail, full-service campground, boat ramp, and museum. If you're not up for the round-trip paddle all the way out to Ossabaw, there's plenty to explore on Red Bird Creek and in the many other waterways closer to the park.

INFORMATION: Ossabaw Island, Department of Natural Resources, P.O. Box 14565, Savannah, GA 31416; 912/262-3173; There's no visitor center or facilities on Ossabaw Island. Fort McAllister State Park (912/727-2339) is the most convenient starting point for trips to the preserve, with a campground, office, water, and rest rooms. A $2 entrance fee is charged at the state park.

MAPS: NOAA 11511; USGS Burroughs, Oak Level, Raccoon Key.

HAZARDS: Part of the route described below follows the Intracoastal Waterway, where boat traffic is often heavy. Fortunately, it's pretty easy to keep out of the main channel. Open water conditions prevail on the Ogeechee River and Ossabaw Sound. Tidal currents are strong. Tidal range: 7 feet.

BASE CAMP: Camping on the island is not permitted. The attractive campground adjacent to Red Bird Creek in Fort McAllister State Park is the only local camping option. Sites cost $12/night and the campground is open year round.

PUT-IN: A boat ramp is located next to the campground in the state park. To get to the park: from I-95 take exit 15. Turn E onto GA-144 and go 6.5 miles to GA-144 SPUR. Turn L and go 2.3 miles to the park entrance.

TAKE-OUT: Same as the put-in.

DAY TRIP: **Tidal Creek to Barrier Island.** *A 24-mile round-trip paddle that meanders along a quiet marsh creek before joining a major tidal river that leads to the Ocean and Ossabaw Island. Birding opportunities are excellent in the marsh and on the island. Difficulty rating: 4.*

If you're not up for a full day's paddle out to the island, this trip can be shorted by sticking to the scenic confines of Red Bird Creek. Trips out to Ossabaw I. cannot be completed in a day unless timed to coincide with the tides, as the trip is long and currents are very strong.

Put in at the boat ramp in Fort McAllister SP. Follow the winding route of Red Bird Creek 3.5 miles through an expansive salt marsh to the Florida Passage, a part of the Intracoastal Waterway between Bear River and the Ogeechee River. Turn L and paddle 1 mile to the Ogeechee River. Enter the Ogeechee and follow the R bank as it curves around to the E. Keep close to the R bank as you paddle down river to Bradley Point on Ossabaw Island, a distance of 6 miles. You can land on the sandy point or paddle a short distance around to the Ocean side and follow the long, sandy beach for as far as you like. Chances are good that you'll have the island just about to yourself. Be sure to leave yourself enough time for the return paddle. Retrace your route back to the boat ramp on Red Bird Creek.

Sapelo Island
North River ◊ Doboy Sound

Sapelo Island occupies the exact midpoint of Georgia's Atlantic Coast. The 9-mile-long island, separated from the mainland by a broad expanse of salt marsh cut by tidal rivers and creeks, has a wealth of natural habitats and a rich cultural tradition that dates back more than 3,000 years and continues to flourish in the present. Its position in the middle of the Georgia coast is appropriate, because the island lies somewhere between the extremes of Georgia's wildest barrier islands such as Wassaw and Ossabaw, and those that have been tamed by modern settlements, such as Jekyll and St. Simon's. Sapelo is home to a small settlement of African Americans whose roots on the island date back more than a century, yet most of it remains untouched by human hands.

The Guale Indians were the first people to settle Sapelo, and they were undoubtedly attracted by the same riches that continued to draw people to the island into the twentieth century: a mild climate, amazingly fertile waters for fishing and harvesting mollusks and crustaceans, soil suitable for crop production, and easy access to the mainland and other ports. Like many parts of the southeastern coast, the island changed hands numerous times among the Spanish, French, and British, before finally becoming the possession of the newly constituted United States. For most of the nineteenth and twentieth centuries the island was privately owned and during that time inhabitants farmed the land and fished the estuarine and ocean waters. One of the more recent owners, Richard J. Reynolds, Jr., envisioned a potential for scientific research on the island and laid the foundation for the University of Georgia Marine Institute. Since then most of the island has been allowed to revert to a natural state, and its habitats have been used for study, rather than agricultural production.

The exception to this is Hog Hammock, a 400-acre community of approximately 65 African Americans who trace their lineage directly to the slaves who worked the island's plantations in the first half of the nineteenth century. Guided tours of the village are

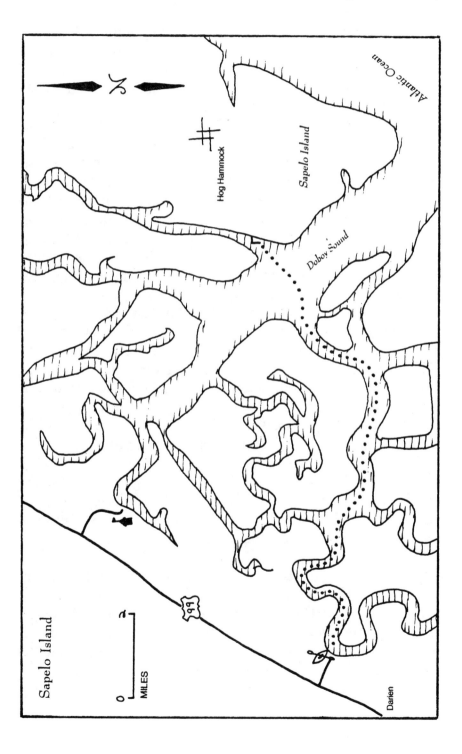

Sapelo Island

led by the residents, and lodging, food, and camping facilities are available to visitors by prior arrangement. Since most of the island is operated as a wilderness preserve and research facility closed to the public, only the residents of Hog Hammock and their guests are allowed on the island's interior.

Day trips to the island are possible, but the paddle out and back is arduous, especially if it isn't timed to take advantage of the tide. Overnight trips are preferable, since they will allow you to take your time and spend a night in Hog Hammock. Camping on the island except as a guest of one of the residents of the community is not permitted. Giving yourself two days will also permit you to adequately explore some of Sapelo's natural and cultural heritage. On the island's interior majestic live oaks trail loose tatters of Spanish moss from long limbs; extensive dunes are overgrown with coastal shrub thickets and sea grasses; a sandy beach extends for miles along the Atlantic; and gulls and sanderlings skitter across the sand at water's edge. Two of plantation-owner Thomas Spalding's architectural achievements still stand: a mansion that was built somewhat after the style of Jefferson's Monticello and renovated after falling into disrepair in the years after the Civil War, and the Long Tabby, Spalding's plantation headquarters. Both buildings were constructed of tabby, a curious mixture of oyster shells, sand, lime, and water.

Sapelo's low-key combination of nature preserve and living museum make it one of the most rewarding destinations for kayakers paddling the Georgia coast. More advance planning is necessary than at many other locations, but the extra effort is amply rewarded by the unique world of Sapelo Island.

INFORMATION: Sapelo Island Visitor Center, P.O. Box 15, Darien, GA 31327; 912/437-3224. The visitor center, located on the mainland just N of Darien, is open Tu–F 7:30 am to 5:30 pm, Sa 8 am to 5:30 pm, and Su 1:30 to 5:00 pm Inside you can pick up maps, brochures, or a listing of camping possibilities on the island. Rest rooms and water are inside.

MAPS: NOAA 11510, USGS Ridgeville, Doboy Sound, Cabretta Inlet.

HAZARDS: Commercial and private fishing boats ply the route from the mainland to the island, which also crosses the Intracoastal Waterway. The combination of strong tidal currents and wind can make paddling against an ebbing or flooding tide just about impossible. Tidal range: 7 feet.

BASE CAMP: You can camp on the island, but only at one of several private camping areas run by the residents of Hog Hammock and only by prior permission. A list of the campgrounds with phone numbers is available from the visitor center. On the mainland, a handful of hotels, motels, and B&Bs are available in Darien.

PUT-IN: From Darien, turn N onto GA-99 (Ridge Rd) and go 3.3 miles to Blue 'N Hall Rd. (To reach the mainland visitor center continue ahead 4.2 miles to Landing Rd. Turn R and go 0.8 miles to the elevated building). Turn R and go 0.5 mile to the boat ramp. From I-95 (exit 11), Blue 'N Hall Rd is 13.2 miles S on GA-99.

TAKE-OUT: Same as the put-in.

DAY TRIP/WEEKENDER: *Sapelo Island Excursion. A 14-mile round-trip paddle down tidal rivers and across a sound to the island. The trip can be paddled as a long day trip or over 2 days, with camping or lodging accommodations available in the community of Hog Hammock. Difficulty rating: 4.*

Strong tidal currents and frequently windy conditions make it advisable to time your trip so that you're paddling with the tide. From the boat ramp, paddle E down the North River, which follows a winding route that twists and doubles back on itself as it meanders through vast expanses of salt marsh. At 3.75 miles you reach the confluence with Back River. Turn NNE and continue paddling out the North River (the L channel). Following the river's L bank you reach the open expanse of Doboy Sound after 1.5 miles. Paddle ENE across the sound 1.25 miles to the mouth of

Duplin River and Sapelo Island. Enter the river and follow the R bank 0.5 mile to the ferry landing and dock. If you're spending the night, your host will meet you at the dock and transport you to the camping area. On day 2, you may want to paddle out around to the Atlantic side of the island, where there's a long, sandy beach. When you're ready to return to the mainland, retrace your route back to the boat ramp at the end of Blue 'N Hall Rd.

Altamaha River

Altamaha River ◊ Darien River

Mention the Altamaha to people outside of Georgia, and odds are good that they'll answer you with only blank looks or raised eyebrows. The name is hardly a geographic commonplace like, say, the Mississippi, the Hudson, or the Potomac. Despite its relative obscurity, the Altamaha is Georgia's largest river and drains an area larger than all but one other river on the East Coast. It begins in the Piedmont at the confluence of a pair of other rivers that flow down out of the Appalachian Mountains—the Oconee and the Ocmulgee. From there it flows languorously for almost 140 miles before dividing into several different channels and emptying into the Atlantic Ocean. The river's apparent lazy pace and lack of whitewater disguise a tremendous force: 100,000 gallons of water per *second* flow out of the Altamaha.

The historic port town of Darien sits on its banks not far from its mouth, and though the town today has an air of lazy, somewhat disheveled gentility, it was once one of the busiest ports on the south Atlantic coast. That was in the days before railroads and automobiles, when the wealth of the Georgia interior—cotton, tobacco, timber, and rice—began its journey to distant ports by being floated down the Altamaha to the sea. The river still plays an important commercial role in the local economy, a fact attested to by the line of shrimp boats tied up on the Darien waterfront. The tidal portion of the river forms a vast estuary, one of the most fertile natural environments on the planet.

The trip described below follows the river as it passes through several distinct environments. At the upstream put-in, the river's banks are blanketed in a lush bottomland forest of bald cypresses and hardwoods. As the river flows downstream and meets the salt water coming in on the tides, the trees give way to the vast wetland prairie of a salt marsh. Here the river channel breaks up into several braids, each one following a different winding course through the tall, wheat-colored grasses. This diversity of habitats supports a stunning diversity of flora and fauna, including 125 endangered or threatened species. Near the start of the trip you'll

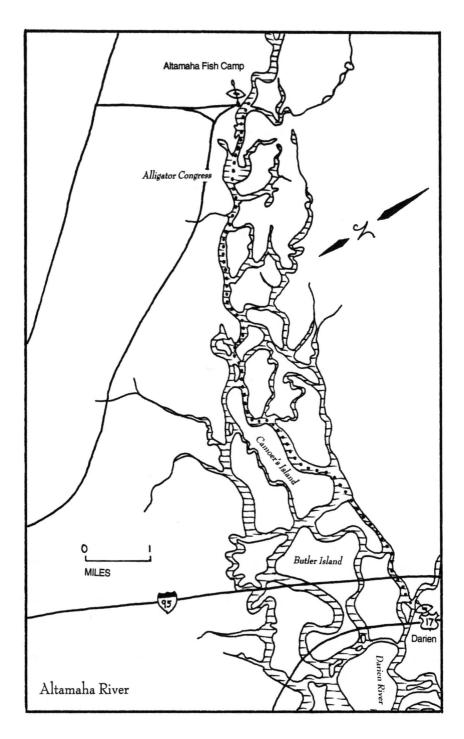

Altamaha Fish Camp

Alligator Congress

MILES

Camoer's Island

Butler Island

Darien River

Darien

Altamaha River

almost certainly see alligators, who favor fresh water, basking in the sun. One small island even has the fanciful name Alligator Congress. A river otter might be playing near the banks, or a deer drinking at river's edge. Downstream species are more adapted to the brackish waters of the marsh. Here wading birds are observed in their highest concentrations, and manatees sometimes break the surface for air.

Paddling the river requires a little more planning and effort than many of the other destinations in this guide, since there's no state or national park along its course to provide a base. Public boat ramps are located at regular intervals for most of the river's length, but facilities are limited. A natural resource as valuable and unique as the Altamaha needs protection, and state agencies and the Nature Conservancy have been working together to preserve the river and the wetlands it drains.

INFORMATION: Altamaha River Bioreserve (Nature Conservancy of Georgia), P.O. Box 484, Darien, GA 31305; 912/437-2161; www.tnc.org/infield/preserve/altamaha. Although the Nature Conservancy has been working for 20 years to protect the river and owns almost 7,000 acres of surrounding habitat, it is not an official information or management contact. If you have questions about paddling or fishing the river, try asking the folks at the Altamaha Fish Camp next to the put-in—they know the river as well as anyone. Supplies are available there too.

MAPS: USGS Cox, Ridgeville, Darien.

HAZARDS: Although anglers in power boats are a common sight on the river, traffic is relatively light. A large-scale topo map is essential to navigate the river's many channels and to avoid entering cuts and blind creeks. Tidal range: 8 feet at the river's mouth; gradually decreases as you move upriver.

BASE CAMP: There's a riverside campground next to the put-in at the Altamaha Fish Camp (912/264-2342). It's open year round and sites cost $12/night. Hotel, motel, and B&B accommodations are available in Darien. Call the Darien Welcome Center (912/437-4192) for listings.

PUT-IN: From I-95, take exit 7B. Turn N onto US-25/US-341 and go 13.6 miles to Altamaha Park Rd. Turn R and go 3.5 miles to a small park and boat ramp.

TAKE-OUT: There's a small boat ramp in town on the Darien River. In downtown Darien, turn W onto Broad St just before the bridge that crosses the river. The boat ramp is at the bottom of the first lane on the L.

DAY TRIP: *Altamaha Estuary. This 17-mile journey begins where the river flows quietly through swamp forests, but travels mostly through the vast marshlands that surround the river on its lower stretches. It ends in the historic town of Darien. Difficulty rating: 3.*

Although the first part of this trip follows the main channel of the river, it soon becomes only a loosely structured paddle, as the river's numerous branches and cuts give the paddler a handful of options. At the put-in, the tidal range is only a foot or two; at Darien it's just under 8 feet—try to time your trip to take advantage of the ebb tide.

Put in at the boat ramp next to the Altamaha Fish Camp and head down the river. For the first half of the trip the river channel is relatively straight and easy to follow, flowing through bottomland swamp forest and past sandhill hammocks. Near the halfway point, the channel splits above Camoer's Island. Take the L channel and paddle past Lewis Island on the L; the swamp forest that covers it has cypresses that are 1,000 years old. Just past the Island Lewis Creek flows in from the L and a narrow cut appears ahead. Paddle into the cut, which joins the Darien River after 1.5 miles. Continue straight down the Darien River 2 miles to the take-out river L just before the US-17 bridge.

Okefenokee National Wildlife Refuge

Suwannee River ◊ Suwannee Canal

The Okefenokee Swamp is one of those mythical, mysterious places that evokes the Old South. The vast interior wetland—the refuge encompasses 650 square miles—is the largest remaining tract of a habitat that was common across much of the Southeast's coastal plain just 200 years ago. Early settlers in the region viewed the water-logged, mosquito-infested, dense swamp forests as unmanageable wastelands, however, and set about to tame them. Massive projects were undertaken to convert the swamps to productive farmland; elaborate networks of canals to drain the land were constructed and the forests were logged. That fate escaped the Okefenokee when the company formed to drain it went bankrupt after having built only about 20 miles of canals. Large tracts of the swamp were subsequently logged, however; the towering cypresses that were felled were as many as 2,000 years old. Fortunately, in 1937 the Okefenokee National Wildlife Refuge was established, ensuring that the magical wilderness would be left intact.

Four major natural habitats coexist in the swamp: hardwood swamp forest, wet prairie, lake, and floating island. The Indians named the region Okefenokee, or trembling earth since the ground of the unstable islands would shift under their feet. The habitats are home to an astonishing variety and abundance of wildlife, both fauna and flora. The most prevalent biological community is the swamp forest, home to the majestic bald cypresses and the beards of Spanish moss that hang from their grey limbs. The largest expanses of wet prairie are on the refuge's eastern side. These open landscapes offer the best opportunity to view the myriad avian species that inhabit the swamp: sandhill cranes, anhingas, wood storks, great blue herons, wood ducks, ospreys, kestrels, teals, ibises, and woodpeckers are just a handful of the 200 different species that can be observed here.

Among the larger fauna, alligators are the most prevalent and most commonly seen, since more than 10,000 of the ancient reptiles inhabit the refuge. Look for them basking in the sun along

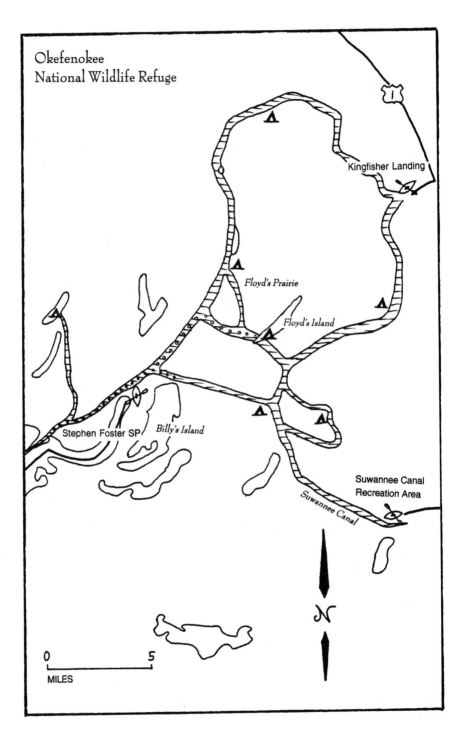

the perimeter of waterways and lakes. Black bears are also abundant in the Okefenokee, though they're much more people-shy and likely to escape detection. White-tailed deer, bobcat, river otter, and fox are among the other mammals that dwell in the swamp.. Six species of poisonous snake live here as well, though they're not aggressive unless startled or provoked.

There are several different ways to explore the Okefenokee, including short hiking trails and a wildlife drive, but none can compare to paddling the intricate network of waterways in a canoe or kayak. Only these human-powered, shallow-draft vessels can take you into the heart of the swamp and get you close to its wildlife without scaring it off. Six connecting water trails cover 107 miles that pass through all of the refuge's natural habitats. Day trips are possible from any of the three main entrances, but only a trip of two days or more, with at least one night spent in the backcountry, will permit you to begin to fully experience all the sights, sounds, and scents of the Okefenokee. Restrictions are tight on the number of people permitted to camp on the refuge at any given time, and advance planning is required. Backcountry camping permits are required can be reserved up to two months in advance.

There are four different access points to the Okefenokee. Three of these are park-like settings with facilities and access to the canoe trails: Suwannee Canal Recreation Area (E), Okefenoke Swamp Park (N), and Stephen Foster State Park (W). Both trips described below begin in Stephen Foster State Park, but with a refuge map you can plan your own itinerary that begins and/or ends at any of the three entrances.

INFORMATION: Okefenokee National Wildlife Refuge, Route 2, Box 3330, Folkston, GA 31537; 912/496-3331; www.gorp.com/gorp /resource/us_nwr/ga_okefe.htm. An entrance fee of $5/vehicle is charged at the NWR. Water, rest rooms, a pay phone, refuge maps and brochures, and some supplies are available at Stephen C. Foster State Park (912/637-5274).

MAPS: USGS Billy's Island, The Pocket.

HAZARDS: Motorized boats are permitted on some of the day-use trails, but they don't pose much of a problem. The main hazards in the refuge are those normally associated with remote backcountry travel in a southern swamp: insects, alligators, and poisonous snakes. Only insects attack without provocation.

BASE CAMP: Stephen C. Foster State Park has the only car-accessible campground at the refuge. Sites cost $12–15/night depending on the season. To really experience the Okefenokee, however, you'll want to spend at least one night in the backcountry. This requires some advance planning, as camping in the refuge is strictly regulated. Only one party per night is allowed at each of the 7 sites. Reservations must be made in advance, and are accepted up to 2 months ahead of the date you plan to camp. Call 912/496-3331 weekdays between 7 am and 10 am. In March and April sites are usually taken the first day they become available, so call early.

PUT-IN: There are 3 different access points to the Okefenokee and NWR. Both trips described below begin at the Stephen Foster SP entrance. To get there: from I-10 take exit 47. Turn N onto CO-125 and go 9.7 to CO-127. Turn R and go 9.9 miles to FL-2. Turn L and go (at 15 miles enter GA where the road becomes GA-94) 23.3 miles to GA-177. Turn R and go 17 miles to the park visitor center and boat access. Launch fee is $1.

TAKE-OUT: Same as the put-in for the trips below, though one-way trips are possible to either of the other access areas.

DAY TRIP: *Billy's Island/Suwannee River Sill Exploration. A 14-mile round-trip paddle that offers a glimpse of swamp forest habitat and the wildlife it supports. Difficulty rating: 1.*

From the put-in, paddle out the short canal to the Suwannee River. Turn R and paddle upstream against the mild current 2.5 miles to Billy's Island. There's a boat landing here and a nature trail on the island. After you've explored the island, retrace your route back to the head of the canal. You can either stop back at the state park for lunch, or continue on to the second leg of the route. Continue down the Suwannee River to a section called the Narrows. The current picks up here a bit, something to keep in mind for the return trip, when you'll be paddling against it. After 5 miles you reach the "sill," a berm that runs from the forest uplands outside the refuge to Pine Island. When you're ready to return, retrace your route back to the put-in.

WEEKENDER: *Swamp, Prairie, Island. A-16-mile round-trip paddle with an overnight at an old hunting cabin on Floyd's Island. Trip highlights are the chance to paddle through several of the refuge's natural habitats and the eerie isolation and vivid night music of the swamp after dark. Difficulty rating: 2.*

The entire route is blazed with red, then green canoe icons. From the put-in paddle out the short feeder canal. Turn R and paddle 2 miles to a junction. Turn L and paddle 4 miles to another junction just past Minnie's Lake. Turn R and paddle 2 miles past Floyd's Prairie to Floyd's Island, where the cabin is located.

On day 2 retrace your route back to the put-in. Longer trips are possible by continuing along the red or green trail. You can choose a route that either returns to the state park or ends at the Kingfisher Landing entrance.

Cumberland Island National Seashore

Crooked River ◊ Cumberland Sound ◊ Brickhill River ◊ Atlantic Ocean

Cumberland Island is the southernmost in the string of barrier islands, known collectively as the Sea Islands, that line the Georgia Coast. Encompassing more than 15,000 acres, it is also the largest of the islands and the most popular of those preserved in a primitive or semi-primitive state. The island, an additional 17,000 acres of salt marsh, and a small parcel of land in St. Mary's comprise the national seashore. Unconnected to the mainland by any roadway, Cumberland Island can only be reached by boat, a circumstance that limits the number of visitors. A ferry runs regularly between St. Mary's and the southern end of the island, which is where most park service facilities are located.

The majority of the island exists today in a wild state, but human settlement there dates back more than a thousand years and continued into the much more recent past. Shell middens attest that Native Americans were the island's earliest inhabitants. After them, the Spanish briefly controlled the region, then the British, who built forts on the island, and finally the Americans. Evidence of the earliest settlements are scant, but the ruins of an eighteenth-century home built by the widow of Revolutionary War general Nathanael Greene can be toured and a later building, a Georgian Revival mansion built by steel magnate Andrew Carnegie, still stands, though in a rather dilapidated condition.

A narrow dirt lane runs the length of the island beneath the arching limbs of massive live oaks draped with gossamer strands of Spanish moss. The maritime forest, which covers much of the island's interior, is one of the most beautiful and haunting on the Georgia coast. Like all barrier islands, Cumberland is home to several other major biological communities as well. The most extensive—and ecologically important—is the salt marsh that sprawls across thousands of acres on the island's sound side. Here wetland prairies of tall, golden grass are cut by narrow tidal creeks and bordered by larger rivers and sounds. An astonishingly large percentage of marine life is born and nurtured here, a fact that accounts for the hundreds of wading birds and shore birds

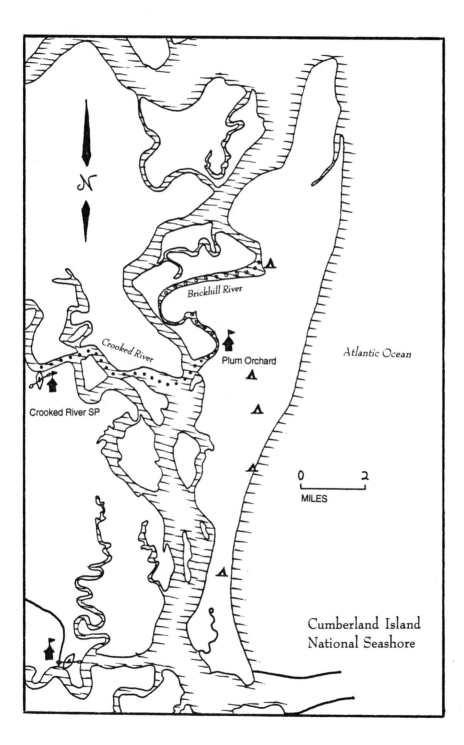

Brickhill River

Crooked River

Plum Orchard

Crooked River SP

Atlantic Ocean

0   2
MILES

Cumberland Island
National Seashore

that rely on the marsh for their own sustenance. At the other side of the island, a long beach of fine sand stretches the entire length of the island. Relatively barren from an ecological point of view, this habitat is perhaps most appreciated by human visitors, who use it for sunbathing, swimming, and walking beside the Atlantic waves. Behind the beach are the dunes, held in place by the root systems of sea oats and other coastal plants. Boardwalks have been placed at regular intervals to keep visitors off the dunes and so help protect them.

These varied natural habitats foster a great diversity of flora and fauna. Aside from insect and plant species, birds are the most visible and abundant lifeform. Song birds in the shadowed hush of the maritime forest, shore birds on the long beach and soaring above the waves, and wading birds in the salt marsh. In both the ocean and the sound dolphins can sometimes be seen breaking the surface; Loggerhead sea turtles use the beach as a nesting ground each summer; and white-tailed deer and raccoons prowl the forests at dusk in search of food.

Although many different kinds of boat moor at the island's dock, none is as well suited as a kayak for navigating the island's myriad waterways or exploring its natural habitats. Only a kayak will take you within feet of a great blue heron without arousing its suspicion or allow you to land on the beach or on a strip of firm land beside the salt marshes. And with a handful of wilderness camping areas on the island, trips of two or more days are easy to plan. In fact, you'll need at least two days to even begin to adequately explore the rich historical and natural heritage of Cumberland Island.

INFORMATION: Cumberland Island National Seashore, P.O. Box 806, St. Marys, GA 31558; 912/882-4336; www.nps.gov/cuis. The visitor center, located at the end of GA-40 in St. Mary's (9.1 miles E of I-95, exit 2), is open daily from 8:15 am to 4:30 pm. Inside you can get maps, guide books, and camping permits. A $4 day-use fee is required to visit the island.

MAPS: NOAA 11489 ; USGS Harrietts Bluff, Cumberland Island North, Cumberland Island South, Fernandina Beach.

HAZARDS: Small commercial fishing boats and pleasure craft of various sorts are fairly common on the rivers and sounds behind the islands. Tidal currents are strong, and, at confluences and inlets, unpredictable. Tidal range: 6.5 feet at the inlets.

BASE CAMP: Cumberland Island may offer the best camping deal on the Georgia coast. There's a developed campground on the island, as well as 4 primitive camping areas, 2 of which are ideally located for overnight paddling trips. Camping at one of the backcountry sites costs $2/night and a permit must be picked up from the visitor center in advance (912/882-4335). Advance reservations are accepted. There's water at the sites, but it must be treated for drinking. The developed campground has drinking water and rest rooms with showers. If you'd rather camp on the mainland, Crooked River State Park has sites that cost $12/night and are available year round.

PUT-IN: Both trips described below begin at Crooked River State Park. From I-95 take exit 2. Turn E onto GA-40 and go 2.4 miles to GA-40 SPUR. Turn L and go 6.2 miles to the boat ramp at Crooked River SP. A $2 launch fee is charged.

TAKE-OUT: Same as the put-in.

DAY TRIP: *Destination: Plum Orchard. This 12-mile round-trip takes you past forested uplands and broad salt marshes to the back side of Cumberland Island and the site of one of two Carnegie family mansions on the island that are on the National Register of Historic Places. Difficulty rating: 3.*

Put in at the boat ramp in Crooked River SP. Paddle downriver along the bluffs on the R until the river bends to the L past a large expanse of marshland. The river's course is winding, but good maps and the strong tidal flow should keep you on track. At about the halfway point to the island, a series of small white buoys marks the main channel. As you near the island and the mouth of the Brickhill River, the red-roofed boathouse of Plum Orchard comes into view. Paddle toward it and land next to the dock after about 6 miles. You can pick up a trail map here and wander the grounds or explore the island's interior on the network of hiking trails (it's about 2.5 miles to the beach and Atlantic Ocean). When you're done exploring, retrace your route back to Crooked River SP.

WEEKENDER: *Crooked River to Brickhill Bluff. A 21-mile round-trip paddle down the Crooked River and through the marshes on the back side of Cumberland Island. Highlights are the various natural habitats and the campsites' beautiful setting. Difficulty Rating: 3.*

Follow the directions above under "daytrip" to Plum Orchard and the Brickhill River. Continue up the river for 1.5 miles to the first cut that appears on the R. Enter the cut and follow its winding course through the salt marsh for 1 mile until it rejoins the Brickhill River. Turn R and paddle 2 miles to where the river widens and bends to the L. A narrow beach appears ahead beneath a lush maritime forest. The campsites are in an enchanting setting amidst the stately live oaks. A hand water pump is the only "improvement" to the camping area.

On day 2 take time to explore some of the island on foot. When you're ready to return to the mainland, retrace your route back to the boat ramp at Crooked River SP.

Fort Clinch State Park
Amelia River ◊ Cumberland Sound

Begun in 1847 to protect the entrance to the St. Mary's River, Fort Clinch has stood sentinel at the northern tip of Amelia Island, the northernmost of Florida's barrier islands, ever since. The fort has never seen action, although during the Civil War it was occupied by first Confederate, and then Union troops. Following the war the fort's importance diminished, until 1898 and the Spanish-American War, when it was again fully armed. By 1935 Fort Clinch had been abandoned and in 1938 it became the centerpiece of one of Florida's first state parks.

The brick and earthenwork fort remains in a remarkably good state of repair, and touring the grounds and buildings is a highlight of most visits to the park. The fort is staffed by park rangers dressed in Union uniforms and tending to the duties that were a soldier's lot during the Civil War. Kayakers have the added benefit of being able to paddle in the fort's shadow, tracing the route followed by warships more than a century ago. Other attractions in the park are a campground, hiking and biking trails, and a fishing pier. A long sandy beach on the park's ocean side is a favorite destination of swimmers, sunbathers, and beachcombers. At the park's north end is Cumberland Sound, and the marshes of the Amelia River spread away from the western side.

Kayakers coming to the island park have a variety of paddling options. The most popular destination is the Amelia River, where it's possible to explore the salt marshes and any of the several tidal creeks that branch off from the river, or to paddle along the waterfront of Fernandina Beach. Part of the town is a national historic district that preserves the architectural heritage of the late nineteenth and early twentieth centuries, the town's heyday as a tourist mecca. Heading in the other direction, you can make the short crossing of Cumberland Sound to the south end of Cumberland Island, a national seashore (see separate entry above for more information). Another option is to paddle along the long stretch of beach that fronts the Atlantic Ocean. The long jetty that helps maintain the channel north of Amelia Island makes it

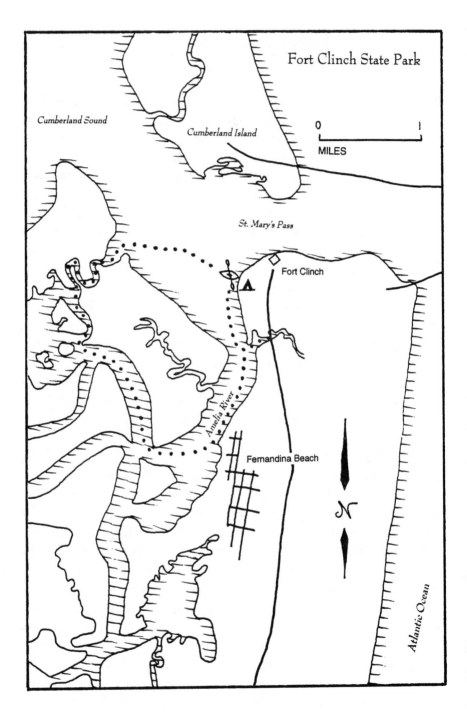

Fort Clinch State Park

Cumberland Sound

Cumberland Island

0   1
MILES

St. Mary's Pass

Fort Clinch

Amelia River

Fernandina Beach

N

Atlantic Ocean

difficult to paddle from the ocean to Cumberland Sound, though the short portage on land is not difficult.

Natural habitats in and around the park include a lush coastal hardwood hammock where palmettos crowd the understory and live oaks draped with Spanish moss provide shade and help create the forest's hushed atmosphere. The park's eastern side is dominated by the long Atlantic beach and a network of massive dunes that rise behind it. The salt marsh that extends west from the island to the mainland harbors dozens of birds, who feed on the abundant marine life in the shallow mud flats.

INFORMATION: Fort Clinch State Park, 2601 Atlantic Avenue, Fernandina Beach, FL 32034; 904/277-7274; www.dep.state.fl.us /parks/northeast/clinch.html. The park entrance fee is $3.25 per vehicle. Water and rest rooms are available in the park, as are park maps and brochures.

MAPS: NOAA 11503, USGS Fernandina Beach.

HAZARDS: Currents in Cumberland Sound are strong and unpredictable. The St. Mary's Entrance is a major shipping channel, so be prepared for some traffic. Tidal range: 6 feet.

BASE CAMP: The developed car campground in the state park can serve as an ideal base for exploring the area. The campground is open year round and sites cost $12–17/night, depending on the season. Backcountry camping is available at designated sites on Cumberland Island National Seashore (see separated entry above for details).

PUT-IN: From I-95, take exit 129. Turn E onto A1A and go 14.3 miles to Atlantic Ave. Turn R and go 1.5 miles to the park entrance, L. Boats can be launched from an access area at the end of the campground road.

TAKE-OUT: Same as the put-in.

DAY TRIP: *Historic Fort and Tidal Marsh Tour. This 8-mile paddle provides a chance to view Fort Clinch from the water and to explore the environments of a tidal creek and salt marsh. Difficulty rating: 3.*

Launch your kayak from the small sandy landing at the end of the campground road. Paddle S for less than a mile to the entrance to Egan Creek on the L. Turn into the narrow creek and paddle a short distance to where the park road crosses overhead. Near here was the original settlement of Fernandina Beach, the layout and foundations of which can still be seen. Turn around and paddle back out to the mouth of the creek. Turn S and paddle 1 mile to the Fernandina Beach waterfront. The town was relocated here when it became the site of the northern terminus of the railroad. The historic district, which is the site of many 100-year-old houses of architectural merit, is well worth exploring on foot. Follow the river as it curves away from the town and is joined by Lanceford Creek. Turn N into the first wide cut and paddle 1.5 miles to an entrance to Tiger Creek, R. Turn into the creek and follow its winding route N to Cumberland Sound, about 2 miles away. When you reach the open waters of the sound, turn E and paddle 1.5 miles back to the boat launch.

St. Augustine
Matanzas River ◊ Salt Run

North America's oldest city is also one of Florida's most attractive. Like all cities before the advent of the railroad and automobile, St. Augustine grew up beside a navigable body of water, in this case Matanzas Bay. It shares another benefit with other pre-twentieth-century metropolises: it was built on a scale designed with walking from place to place in mind. For kayakers these dual facts make St. Augustine an ideal paddling destination. You can approach the city from the water, tie up at the city docks, and then spend an hour or two exploring the historic district before returning to your kayak.

Just 52 years after Ponce de Leon "discovered" Florida, fellow Spaniard Don Pedro Menendez de Aviles founded Florida's first permanent settlement. He chose the location with military operations in mind, and St. Augustine soon became the base for a skirmish with the French, who had built Fort Caroline at the mouth of the St. Johns River. The Spanish won the battle and put to death most of the Frenchmen, giving the river and bay their common name—Matanzas, Spanish for "slaughters."

Over the next three centuries, as the territory changed hands among the Spanish, French, British, and finally, the United States, the strategic location of St. Augustine made it the site of a series of fortifications. The most ambitious of these was the Castillo de San Marcos, built between 1672 and 1695 by the Spanish to protect the city from attacks by the British. The impressive fort, now a national monument open to visitors, still stands near the entrance to the harbor and is the oldest and most impressive of the city's many historic buildings. Like many of St. Augustine's other early buildings, the fort was built from *coquina*, a material made from seashell fragments and lime mortar.

The rest of the historic district is within short walking distance of the fort and city docks, just south of the Bridge of Lions. Many of the oldest buildings, which date from the eighteenth and nineteenth centuries, are located in the Spanish Quarter. The oldest, which dates to 1732, is known, appropriately enough, as

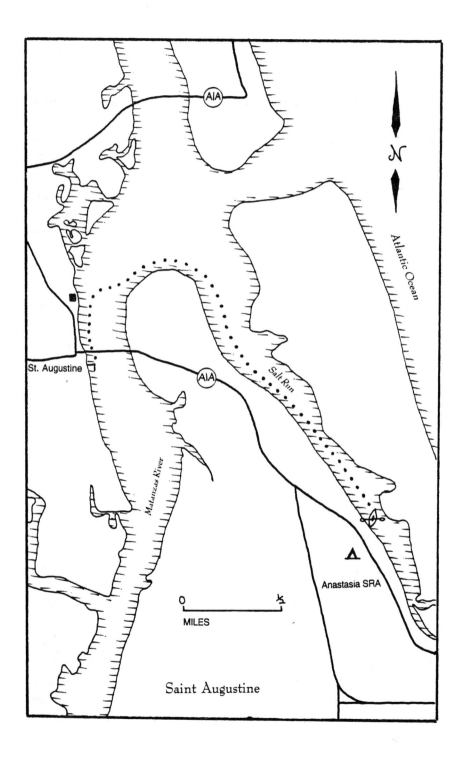

MILES

Anastasia SRA

St. Augustine

Atlantic Ocean

Salt Run

Matanzas River

Saint Augustine

simply the "Oldest House." More recent buildings, such as Flagler College and the Lightner Museum, started out as grand hotels built by railroad magnate Henry Flagler in the 1880s, the earliest days of Florida's tourist industry.

Across the bay and at the southern entrance to the harbor is the Anastasia State Recreation Area. An ideal starting place for paddling trips to St. Augustine, the park occupies a barrier spit with oceanfront beach, lagoon, and maritime forests. There's a campground for overnight stays, and a couple of launching sites for kayaks and other watercraft.

INFORMATION: St Augustine & St. Johns County Visitor Center, 10 Castillo Dr, St. Augustine, FL 32084; 904/825-1000. Anastasia State Recreation Area, 1340-A A1A South, St. Augustine, FL 32084; 904/461-2033. Entrance fee to the rec area is $3.25 per vehicle. Water, rest rooms, and pay phones are available at the SRA and at the city docks.

MAPS: NOAA 11485, USGS St. Augustine.

HAZARDS: St. Augustine overlooks the Matanzas River, part of the Intracoastal Waterway. It's particularly crowded here, with commercial vessels and pleasure boats of all types sharing the waters. Open water conditions prevail, especially beyond the St. Augustine Inlet. Tidal range: 4.5 feet.

BASE CAMP: The Anastasia SRA has a developed year-round campground with showers, rest rooms, and water. Sites cost $12–15/night depending on the season. A wide range of other lodging options, from budget motels to historic inns and B&Bs, is available in St. Augustine. Contact the visitor center for listings.

PUT-IN: The trip below begins in Anastasia State Recreation Area. From downtown St. Augustine, cross the Lions Bridge and go 1.4 miles to Anastasia Park Rd. Turn L and go 0.1 mile to the rec area entrance. There are several launch sites in the rec area.

TAKE-OUT: Same as the put-in.

DAY TRIP: *Ocean Strand to North America's Oldest City. This short round-trip paddle begins amidst the dunes and marshes of Anastasia and Conch islands before passing Castillo de San Marcos and entering the harbor of historic St. Augustine. Difficulty rating: 3.*

Put in at either of the first two launches on Salt Run in the SRA. Paddle out to the natural harbor formed by the confluence of the Matanzas River, Tolomato River, and St. Augustine Inlet, about 2 miles from the put-in. Paddle L around the point of St. Augustine Island and enter the wide Matanzas River across from the Castillo de San Marcos. Cross the river and paddle along the St. Augustine waterfront, where the fort anchors the historic district. Paddle S under the Bridge of Lions to the city marina. If you like you can dock here (check in with the dockmaster first) and get out and explore the town's historic district on foot. When you're ready to return. retrace the same route back to the Anastasia SRA.

Canaveral National Seashore
Mosquito Lagoon ◊ Atlantic Ocean

South of Daytona Beach and just north of Cape Canaveral and the Kennedy Space Center, the 57,600 acres of the national seashore preserve coastal habitats in a nearly pristine state. 24 miles of wide, sandy beach front the crashing surf of the Atlantic. Behind the white sands, sea grapes and saw palmetto cover the dunes in dense thickets and help to keep them anchored. On the other side of this natural barrier is Mosquito Lagoon, a vast estuary that plays the role of nursery for an astonishing variety of marine life. At the lagoon's northern end and all along its eastern edge dozens of small islands crowd together like the pieces of a jigsaw puzzle, separated by a maze of narrow, winding waterways. Some of these islands are mangrove swamps, others are covered by coastal shrubs and pockets of maritime forest.

The importance of these interconnected ecosystems has long been recognized by wildlife biologists, and Canaveral National Seashore and the adjacent Merritt Island National Wildlife Refuge were established to maintain an oasis of wildness along a part of the coast that has been plagued by thoughtless, almost unchecked development over the past fifty years. A sea kayak offers the perfect means to explore this wild, scenic coastal region and to observe the wide range of flora and fauna it supports.

More than 700 different species of plants inhabit the national seashore, along with over 300 avian species. All of the birds common to the south Atlantic coast are present here. Wading birds such as the majestic great blue heron, the white-plumed snowy egret, and the white ibis can be readily observed in the shallow flats on Mosquito Lagoon. On the beach and overhead, you're more likely to see shore birds such as the common laughing gull, willet, or royal tern, or raptors such as the peregrine falcon and red-tailed hawk. Several endangered species also depend on Canaveral's natural habitats: loggerhead sea turtles, wood storks, bald eagles, and manatees are all present at one time of the year or another. Despite the high number of terrestrial lifeforms, it pales in comparison to the abundance of the

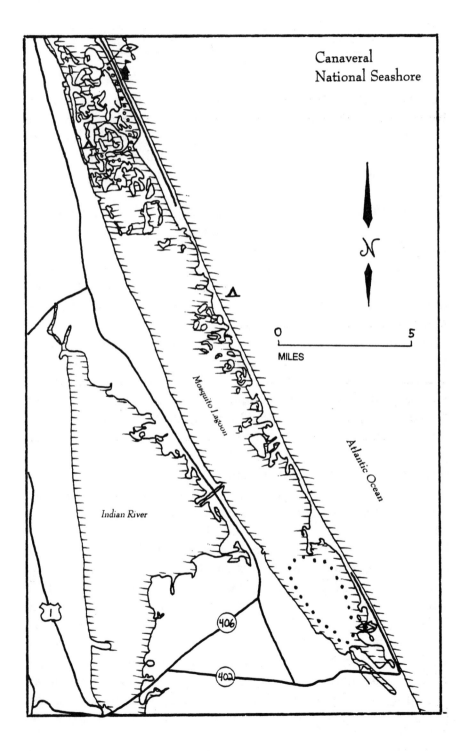

Canaveral
National Seashore

N

0   5

MILES

Mosquito Lagoon

Atlantic Ocean

Indian River

1

406

402

marine world found beneath the surface of the lagoon. Here hundreds of species of fish, crustaceans, and mollusks begin their lives. This very abundance, in fact, is what attracts the birds, who come to prey on them.

Human settlement of the area long predates the arrival of the Spanish in 1513. The Timucan tribe inhabited the region now enclosed by the national seashore for nearly 2,000 years. Although the last members of the tribe had been driven out by the middle of the eighteenth century, a partial record of their culture remains in the burial mounds they left behind. Turtle Mound is one piece of the archaeological record that has been preserved but not yet excavated. One day it will help fill in some of the outlines of the story of the Timucan's way of life.

Kayakers at Canaveral have the option of paddling just beyond the Atlantic waves or on the more sheltered waters of Mosquito Lagoon. While the ocean offers a challenge and the rare opportunity in Florida to follow mile after mile of pristine Atlantic beach, the rough surf here (favored by surfers) puts it beyond the level of novice kayakers. Most paddlers choose to explore the intriguing environs of Mosquito Lagoon anyway. Here you can follow the tortuous waterways that wind among dozens of islands, paddle in the shadow of live oaks draped with Spanish moss, observe dozens of species of birds up close in their natural habitats with a pair of binoculars, or bring a rod and reel and angle for game fish. More than a half dozen backcountry campsites make trips of a weekend or a week possible. A single backcountry site is also available on the Atlantic beach, allowing for multi-day ocean paddles.

Other favorite activities at the seashore are beach combing, swimming, surfing, hiking on several short nature trails, fishing both from a boat and from the beach, and picnicking at one of several picnic areas. Stop in at the visitor center before heading out onto the water for maps, camping permits, and other info.

INFORMATION: Superintendent, Canaveral National Seashore, 308 Julia St., Titusville, FL 32796-3521; 407/267-1110; www.nps.gov /cana. The entrance fee to the park is $5/vehicle. Maps, brochures, and camping permits are available at the visitor center. Rest rooms and water are there too.

MAPS: NOAA 11485; USGS Ariel, Oak Hill, Pardon Island, Wilson.

HAZARDS: A wide range of motorized water craft share the Mosquito Lagoon, including the camouflaged boats of waterfowl hunters in winter. Tidal range: 3.5 feet at the entrance to Canaveral Harbor.

BASE CAMP: Primitive backcountry camping is permitted at any of 9 designated areas, 8 of them on islands in Mosquito Lagoon. A permit, available from the visitor center (904/428-3384), is required. Permits are free and are available up to 7 days in advance. Backcountry sites are undeveloped, without drinking water or toilets.

PUT-IN: For the day trip: from I-95 take exit 80. Turn E onto FL-406 and go 16.3 miles to the Eddy Creek boat ramp, L.
     For the weekender: from I-95, take exit 84. Turn E onto FL-44 and go 4 miles to AIA. Continue straight and drive 10 miles (at 9.4 miles is the boat ramp, R) to the visitor center.

TAKE-OUT: Same as the put-in for both trips.

DAY TRIP: *South End Mosquito Lagoon. This unstructured paddle lets you explore the natural habitats and wildlife of the lagoon estuary. Along the way you might see alligators, river otters, and dozens of species of waterfowl and wading birds. Difficulty rating: 2.*
     Put in at the Eddy Creek boat ramp. After you paddle out of the sheltered confines of the creek you'll be at the S end of the lagoon. Turn NW and explore the back side of the barrier island or head W across the lagoon and paddle beneath the dramatic live oak hammocks that cover the uplands. The lagoon is nursery to oysters, clams, crabs, and dozens of fish species, so you may want to take time out from paddling and try to catch dinner.

WEEKENDER: *The Islands of Mosquito Lagoon. A 2-day, unstructured paddle through the intricate maze of islands that crowd the lagoon's northern end. Aside from the abundant wildlife, the main highlight is the chance to sleep beneath the stars on a remote coastal island. Difficulty rating: 2.*

A good, large-scale map is essential for navigating the narrow waterways among the islands. Put in at the boat ramp just N of the visitor center. The exact route you follow will depend on which campsite you have for the night. Distances from the put-in to the sites range from one to three miles, so you'll have plenty of time to make camp and explore the amazing habitats of this part of the coast. Be sure to include Turtle Mound and Eldora Hammock as part of your route.

On day 2 you can paddle S onto the more open waters of the lagoon and look for dolphins, manatees, and other wildlife, or choose instead to take your time meandering among the hundreds of small islands that support much of the seashore's diverse vegetation.

Merritt Island National Wildlife Refuge

Indian River

Of the 500 national wildlife refuges in the United States, none can compete with Merritt Island for having an unusual beginning. At the height of the Cold War, President Kennedy's administration determined that the United States needed to match and eventually outpace the formidable space program of Russia. Land was acquired on the Florida coast around Cape Canaveral to be used as the site for a space center. NASA kept the lands it needed for a launching pad and support facilities and turned the rest over to the U.S. Fish and Wildlife Service, which used them to create Merritt Island National Wildlife Refuge.

The result is an unusual—and highly successful mix—of space-age technology bordered by some of the richest, most productive wild lands on the entire East Coast. The diversity of wildlife on the 140,000-acre refuge is astonishing, even by the high standards of the subtropical habitats common to the Florida Peninsula. The numbers: 330 bird species, 117 fish species, 65 amphibian and reptile species, and 31 mammal species. Merritt Island is home to more endangered or threatened species than any other refuge in the United States, 21 in all, including the manatee, bald eagle, roseate tern, kemps ridley turtle, loggerhead turtle, magnificent frigatebird, and eastern indigo snake. The diversity of wildlife is tied directly to the diversity of habitats: hardwood hammocks, pine flatwoods, salt and brackish marshes, Atlantic beach, dunes, shrub thickets, fresh-water impoundments, mangrove swamps, citrus groves, and the Indian River.

Kayakers can choose between paddling the Indian River or Mosquito Lagoon (the latter is covered above under Canaveral National Seashore). Or both can be combined on a single trip, since they're connected by a short canal that's part of the Intracoastal Waterway. Only day trips are possible on the refuge, which is only open to visitors during daylight hours. If you want to spend more than a day exploring the region you can camp on one of the backcountry islands or along the beach at Canaveral National Seashore.

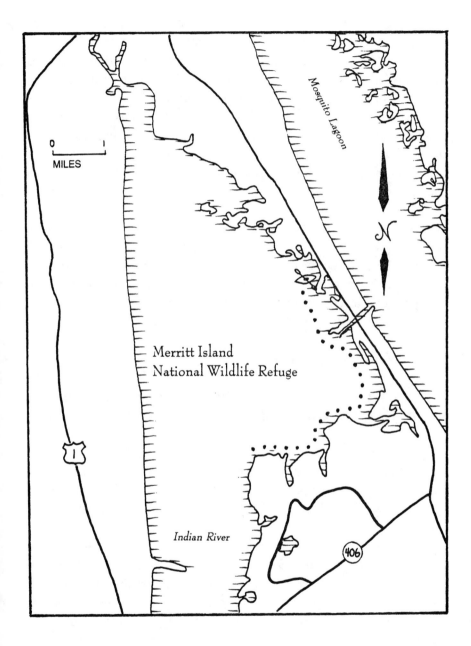

MILES

Mosquito Lagoon

N

Merritt Island
National Wildlife Refuge

Indian River

406

In addition to paddling, the refuge offers opportunities for hiking on several short nature trails, hunting for waterfowl during the appropriate seasons, and fishing for any of the many species of game fish that inhabit refuge waters. But no activity is more popular, or more amply rewarded, than birding. The refuge is located along the Atlantic Flyway, which makes the fall and winter months among the best for viewing the widest variety of birds. But regardless of the season, birders are guaranteed a diversity of species that is unmatched just about anywhere else in the continental United States.

INFORMATION: Refuge Manager, Merritt Island National Wildlife Refuge, P.O. Box 6504, Titusville, FL 32782-6504; 407/861-0667; www.gorp.com/gorp/resource/us_ns/cape.htm. The refuge visitor center is open weekdays 8 am to 4:30 pm and weekends 9 am to 5 pm. Inside you can pick up maps, brochures, and other info. The refuge is only open during daylight hours.

MAPS: USGS Mims, Oak Hill, Wilson.

HAZARDS: With the Intracoastal Waterway and hunters using the waterways in winter, there are plenty of other boats usually on the water.

BASE CAMP: Camping is not permitted on the refuge. Primitive backcountry sites are available at Canaveral National Seashore (see entry above). Hotels and motels are available in Titusville.

PUT-IN: Several boat ramps provide access to refuge waters. To reach the refuge: from I-95 take exit 80. Turn E onto FL-406 and go 5.7 mi to Wildlife Drive (the visitor center is ahead another 2 miles). Turn L and go 8.8 mi to a primitive boat access, L, on the Indian River. A boat ramp on Mosquito Lagoon is located 0.2 mi up the road at the end of a 0.5-mile dirt road, R.

TAKE-OUT: Same as the put-in.

DAY TRIP: *Indian River Exploration. This 13-mile paddle follows the eastern banks of the Indian River. Natural habitats include marshes, cabbage palms, live oak hammock, and stands of pine. The opportunities for birding are outstanding. Difficulty rating: 3.*

From the put-in paddle south along the shoreline. At 1.5 miles you pass the ICW. A subtropical forest covers most of this part of the refuge. Continue south another 2 miles to the mouth of Dummit Creek. You can paddle up the creek about a mile and have a good chance of observing many different species of wildlife. Back out at the creek's mouth turn L and follow the marshy shoreline 3 miles to where it reaches a point and curves away to the S. From here, turn around and retrace your route back to the put-in.

Loxahatchee National Wildlife Refuge
Canoe Trail

Loxahatchee National Wildlife Refuge is located west of the heavily developed strip of beachside resort communities that line the Atlantic coast between Fort Lauderdale and West Palm Beach. The 145,600-acre nature preserve is actually a part of the Everglades, the vast wetland that once occupied the entire southern tip of the Florida Peninsula from Florida Bay to Lake Okeechobee. The once-pristine Everglades have been radically altered over the past two centuries by policies of water management that included the construction of dikes, canals, and levies. The effect has been so deleterious that today the long-term existence of the Everglades is in jeopardy.

The majority of the refuge is given over to four major wetland communities: wet prairies, saw-grass ridges, sloughs, and tree islands. Canals rim the refuge, providing access to anglers and boats. A boardwalk trail provides access to another wetland habitat, a lush cypress forest where colorful epiphytic plants explode from the limbs of trees and suck sustenance from the damp air. Markers along the trail describe the ecology of a swamp forest and provide insight into the symbiotic functioning of the flora and fauna.

Both kayakers and canoeists get better access to the refuge's rich natural habitats than other visitors. A 5.5-mile canoe trail forms a loop that passes through the major biological communities. Wildlife along the trail is abundant. Alligators can be seen sunning themselves at the water's edge, river otters swim through the narrow slough, and wood storks wade through the saw grass prairie. The refuge is particularly rewarding for visitors with an interest in avian species, as more than 250 have been counted here. One animal whose range includes the refuge, but which you almost certainly will not see, is the Florida panther. The most endangered mammal in North America, there are fewer than 30 of the animals left in the wild.

Visitors should begin a trip at the visitor center, where refuge maps and wildlife species lists are available. It's also the starting

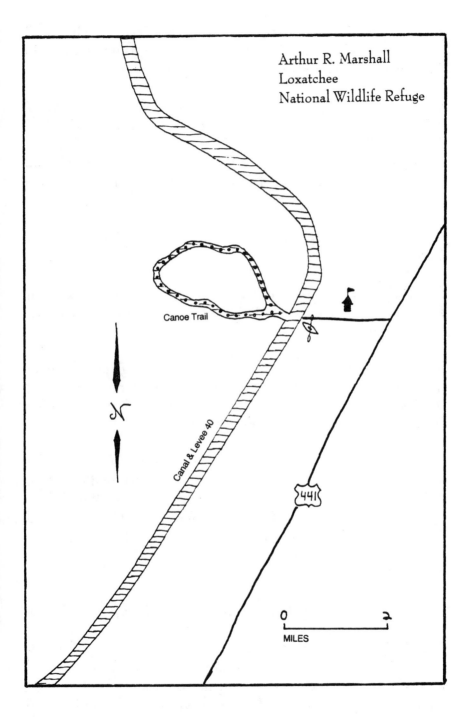

Arthur R. Marshall
Loxatchee
National Wildlife Refuge

Canoe Trail

Canal & Levee 40

441

0   2

MILES

place for the short *Cypress Swamp Boardwalk Trail*, which is well worth the half hour it takes to walk. Camping is not allowed in the refuge, which is only open during daylight hours.

INFORMATION: Refuge Manager, Arthur R. Loxahatchee National Wildlife Refuge, 10216 Lee Rd, Boynton Beach, FL 33437-4796; 407/734-8303; www.gorp.com/gorp/resource/us_nwr/fl_loxah.htm. A $5/vehicle entrance fee is charged. Maps and brochures are available in the visitor center. The refuge is open during daylight hours only.

MAPS: USGS Greenacres City, University Park, Loxahatchee SE, Big Lake.

HAZARDS: Alligators frequently bask by the side of the canoe trail. Paddlers should not come within 15 ft of the animals and should exercise caution.

BASE CAMP: Camping is not permitted on the refuge and there are no public campgrounds in the vicinity. A wide range of hotels, motels, and B&Bs is available in Boynton Beach and the other beach towns that line the Atlantic Ocean.

PUT-IN: A boat ramp is located at the end of the refuge road. To get there from I-95: take exit 52 and turn W onto Boynton Beach Blvd (FL-804). Drive 8 miles (at 6 miles pass under the Florida Turnpike, exit 86) to US-441. Turn L and go 2 miles to Lee Rd. Turn R and go 0.3 mile to the refuge entrance.

TAKE-OUT: Same as the put-in.

DAY TRIP: *Loxahatchee Canoe Trail. A 5.5-mile loop that takes you through some of the remoter wetland habitats that comprise the refuge. The highlight of the trip is the chance to observe a wide range of wildlife, with alligator sightings almost guaranteed. Difficulty rating: 2.*

From the put-in paddle into the narrow waterway behind the sign for the canoe trail. The entire route is signed and easy to follow. Along the way are signboards that describe various features of the local ecology. A platform with pit toilet is also located along the trail. Allow yourself about 3 hours to complete the trail. Much of the narrow trail is shallow and blanketed with lily pads, making going slow. Paddlers with a strong fear of alligators may want to pass on this trip.

The Gulf Coast

The Gulf Coast Key Map

1. Gulf Islands NS
2. St. Andrews SRA
3. St. Joseph Peninsula SP
4. St. Vincent NWR
5. St. George Island SP
6. St. Marks NWR
7. Manatee Springs SP
8. Crystal River SP
9. Cedar Keys NWR
10. Anclote Keys
11. Cayo Costa SP

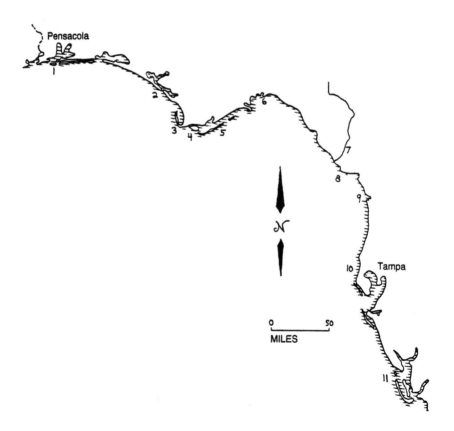

Weather Readings at Pensacola, FL

Month	Air Temp (High F°)	Water Temp F°	Wind Speed (mph)	Wind Direction
January	61°	56°	10.5	N
February	65°	58°	11	N
March	72°	63°	11	N
April	79°	71°	10.5	S
May	85°	78°	9	S
June	90°	84°	8	S
July	91°	85°	7	S
August	91°	86°	7	NE
September	88°	82°	8	NE
October	81°	74°	8.5	N
November	71°	65°	9.5	N
December	64°	58°	10	N

Weather Readings at Naples, FL

Month	Air Temp (High F°)	Water Temp F°	Wind Speed (mph)	Wind Direction
January	76°	66°	9	N
February	77°	66°	9.5	E
March	81°	71°	10	S
April	85°	77°	9.5	ENE
May	88°	82°	9	E
June	90°	86°	8.5	E
July	91°	87°	7.5	E
August	92°	87°	7.5	ENE
September	91°	86°	8	ENE
October	87°	81°	9	NNE
November	82°	73°	9	NNE
December	78°	68°	9	N

Gulf Islands National Seashore
Gulf of Mexico ◊ Big Lagoon

Gulf Islands National Seashore stretches across a 150-mile chain of barrier islands in Mississippi and Florida. The Florida component includes parts of Santa Rosa Island and Perdido Key, as well as a couple of smaller parcels on the mainland. The islands are located just a short distance from the historic city and naval air station of Pensacola. Both islands are accessible by car. The seashore was established in 1971 to achieve several goals, including conservation of important coastal habitats and outdoor recreation for the public in a region where land was becoming a scarce and expensive commodity. The large majority of the national seashore's holdings are on the long, narrow islands that are classic examples of the barrier land masses that help protect coastal mainlands from the harsh effects of violent storms.

For most visitors, the main appeal of the islands is the wide beach of fine white sand that slopes gently to the brilliant blue waters of the Gulf of Mexico. Year after year and on one list after another, these beaches rank among the very best in the nation. After driving past the charmless, blocky masses of resort hotels and condominium complexes that line the route to the seashore's entrance, it becomes clear just what a national treasure these vast empty expanses of island, sea, and sky are.

Aside from the beaches, the natural habitats of Gulf Island National Seashore will be familiar to anyone who has spent time exploring barrier islands. Behind the beach, a network of dunes is held in place against wind and weather by sea oats and shrub thickets. Behind that stands of oak and pine harbor some of the mammals, such as raccoons and opossums, that are native to these habitats. On the back side of the islands you'll find both narrow strips of sand and salt marshes. The latter are an important incubator for marine life and a favorite hunting ground for the many wading and shore birds that inhabit the region.

In addition to their natural heritage, these islands have a historic dimension as well. The Spanish were the first Europeans to settle these shores, first in 1559, and then again in 1698. Over

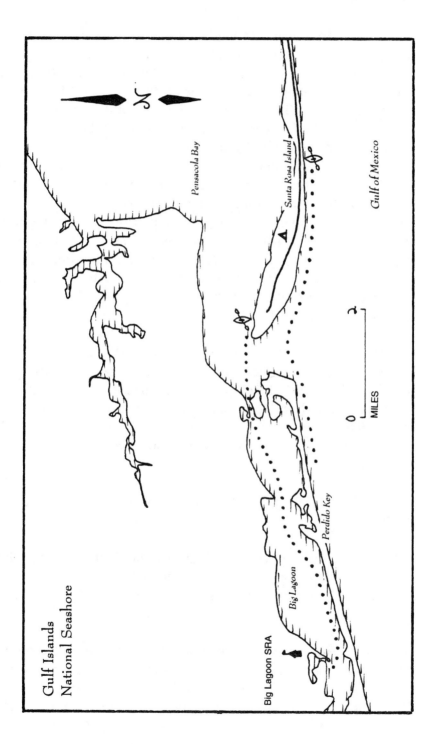

Gulf Islands
National Seashore

Pensacola Bay

Santa Rosa Island

Gulf of Mexico

Big Lagoon SRA

Big Lagoon

Perdido Key

MILES

the next hundred years the land changed hands numerous times among the Spanish, the French, the British, and, finally, the United States. The U.S. had military designs for the area, and built a series of fortifications along the coast. One of these was Fort Pickens, at the western end of Santa Rosa Island. Many of the structures and armaments of the fort can still be seen today, and a museum on the site provides additional information.

For kayakers, the main appeal of Gulf Islands NS is the chance to paddle away from summertime crowds and follow long, empty stretches of some of the most magnificent coast in the country. Birding is also a favorite activity, and a pair of binoculars will be useful for observing some of the almost 300 species of birds that inhabit or pass through the region on annual migrations. A full day is just enough time to explore most of this part of the seashore, but a developed campground makes longer visits possible.

INFORMATION: Superintendent, Gulf Islands National Seashore, 1801 Gulf Breeze Parkway, Gulf Breeze, FL 32561; 904/934-2600; www.nps.gov/guis. The entrance fee is $6/vehicle (valid for one week). Water and rest rooms are located in several places within the NS. The visitor center is located on US-98 1.7 miles E of Gulf Breeze, where you can pick up maps, brochures, and other info. Hours are 9 am to 4 pm.

MAPS: NOAA 11383; USGS Fort Barrancas, Gulf Breeze, Perdido Bay.

HAZARDS: The inlet between Perdido Key and Santa Rosa Island is a fairly busy boating lane, with commercial vessels and pleasure boats both a presence. Currents here are strong and tricky. Tidal range: 1 foot.

BASE CAMP: Primitive backcountry camping is not permitted on the NS. A developed car campground (904/934-2621) is located in a wooded setting not far from the put-in. Tent sites cost $15/night. The campground is open year round. A wide variety of hotels, motels, and B&Bs can be found in Pensacola, Gulf Breeze, and on Santa Rosa Island. For listings contact the Pensacola Visitor Center at 800/874-1234.

PUT-IN: From US-98 in Gulf Breeze turn S onto FL-399 (Pensacola Beach Rd.) and go 1.9 miles across the bridge to the outer beaches. Turn R onto Ft. Pickens Rd and go 3 miles to the entrance station. For day trip 1, use the Langdon beach access. For daytrip 2, drive 6.5 miles from the entrance station to the end of the road. Turn L and drive 0.2 mile to where the road curves around to the L. Park as close as you can to the steps that cross the seawall and carry your kayak the 50 yds or so to the water.

TAKE-OUT: You can use either put-in as an end point for either trip.

DAY TRIP 1: *Island Paradise. A 10–15-mile paddle that takes you along some of the most beautiful beaches in the United States. The main highlight is Perdido Key, where you just might have miles of sandy beach all to yourself. Difficulty rating: 3.*

Put in at the Langdon Beach access. You'll have to portage from the parking lot to the Gulf, a distance of about 100 yards. Launch on the beach and paddle W along the narrow barrier island. After 3 miles you'll reach the inlet to Pensacola Bay. Cross the inlet to Perdido Key, about half a mile away. Exercise caution here, as the current is usually strong and the inlet is a major boating channel. When you reach Perdido Key you're at the eastern end of an undeveloped barrier island that stretches west almost 5 miles before the first road appears. Land anywhere along this section you please. You can explore the island habitats, go for a swim, or just lie on the empty beach. When you're ready to return to the put-in, retrace your route.

DAY TRIP 2: *Barrier Island and Estuary Exploration. A 12-mile trip from the western end of Santa Rosa Island to Big Lagoon State Recreation Area, a prime birding area. A stop on Perdido Key is also a highlight. Difficulty rating: 3.*

Put in on the sound side at the W tip of Santa Rosa Island.

Begin by paddling across the channel between the island and Perdido Key. The channel isn't very wide—about half a mile—but the currents are trick and boat traffic always seems to be present. Once you enter Big Lagoon behind Perdido Key the water calms considerably. From the entrance it's about a 5.5 mile paddle due W to the Big Lagoon SRA. Along the way you'll paddle between pristine Perdido Key and intermittent residential developments along the mainland waterfront. As you near the SRA, look for the tall observation tower and use it as a landmark. You can climb the tower for an exceptional panoramic view of the region. There are hiking trails and picnic areas in the SRA. Once you've explored the area's habitats and had some lunch, retrace your route back to Santa Rosa Island. Be sure to leave some time for a visit to Perdido Key. There are plenty of sandy landings on the back side, and from there it's only a short walk to the Gulf side and one of the most magnificent, deserted beaches in the United States.

St. Andrews State Recreation Area
Grand Lagoon ◊ St. Andrew Bay ◊ Gulf of Mexico

Busy St. Andrews State Recreation Area is located at the eastern end of the popular summertime resort of Panama City Beach. After you drive pass the seemingly endless row of hotels pressed up against the soft white sands of the Gulf Coast, you reach the quieter world of this 1,260-acre nature preserve and outdoor recreation destination. The beach is still the highlight here, but a campground, two nature trails, a fishing pier, and boat ramp offer additional possibilities for outdoor recreation.

For kayakers, the boat ramp and access to the Gulf provides a starting point for explorations of even more remote and wild destinations. For in truth, most paddlers seeking solitude and undisturbed natural habitats will find even the recreation area too crowded and noisy. But less than a half mile away is the pristine beauty of Shell Island, an undeveloped, uninhabited barrier island cut off from the mainland by St. Andrews Bay. The only way to reach the island is by boat, and though the rec area runs a shuttle every half hour during summer, the small groups of visitors tend to cluster along a short stretch of the 6.5-mile island.

Shell Island is home to the biological communities common to most barrier islands: wide sandy beach, extensive dune system anchored by sea oats, forest of pines and hardwoods, shrub thicket, and salt marsh. Gulls, pelicans, terns, willets, and dozens of other shore birds can be seen on the island's Gulf side. Bottle-nosed dolphins sometimes visit and can be seen arcing gracefully above the water's surface. White-tailed deer emerge from the woodlands now and then to walk across the dunes or along the beach. Armadillos inhabit the dunes.

Camping is not permitted on Shell Island, so paddlers will have to be content with day visits. With beachside campsites in St. Andrews SRA, however, multi-day excursions are easy enough to undertake. Most visitors to the island are content to spend their time sunning themselves on the snow-white sands of the beach or swimming in the Gulf's turquoise waters. Kayakers with a naturalist bent may want to explore the island's other habitats.

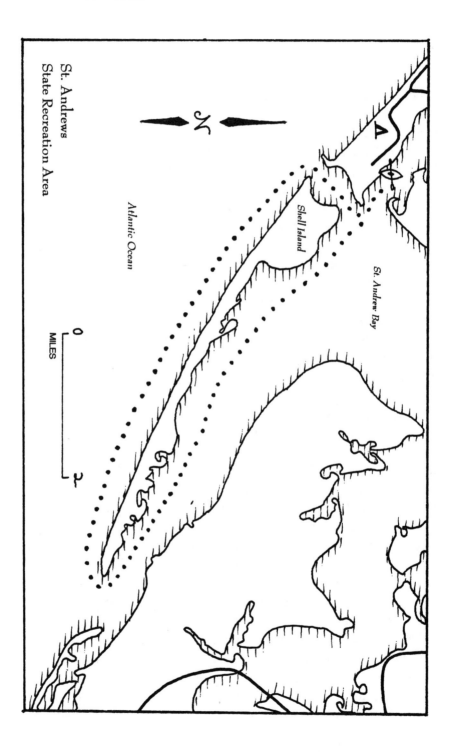

Since these ecosystems are extremely fragile, it's probably a better idea to use the nature trails in the rec area to get an up close view of the flora and fauna of a barrier island.

INFORMATION: St. Andrews State Recreational Area, 4607 State Park Lane, Panama City Beach, FL 32408; 904/233-5140; www. dep.state.fl.us/parks/northwest/andrews.html. The park charges a $4/vehicle entrance fee. Water and rest rooms are available in the park.

MAPS: NOAA 11391; USGS Beacon Beach, Panama City.

HAZARDS: Currents are strongest in the channel between the rec area and Shell Island and require caution. Be particularly careful as you navigate between the jetties at the head of the channel. Boats are also a concern as they shuttle between St. Andrew Bay and the Gulf. Tidal range: 1.5 feet.

BASE CAMP: The car campground inside the SRA makes an ideal base for exploration of Shell Island and the Gulf. It's open year round. Sites cost $16/night from March 1 to September 30, $8/night during the off season. A camp store sells a small selection of supplies. Camping is not allowed outside of the designated sites or on Shell Island. A dizzying array of hotels and motels is available in Panama City Beach.

PUT-IN: From Panama City, drive W on US-98 for about 2 miles (0.7 miles past the bridge) to CO-3031. Turn L and go 3.6 miles to Thomas Dr. Turn L and go 0.5 mile to the entrance. To reach the boat ramp turn L at the camp store and go to the end of the road.

DAY TRIP: *Shell Island Exploration. This paddle can range from a 5-mile out-and-back trip to the island's Gulf beach to a 15-mile circumnavigation of the island. Highlights are the pristine beach and natural habitats on Shell Island. Difficulty rating: 3.*

Put in at the SRA boat ramp and paddle SE for a half mile out of Grand Lagoon to St. Andrew Bay. Turn R around the point and paddle out through the channel between a pair of jetties. As you near the head of the channel keep to the L side and then paddle around to the long, sandy beach and aquamarine waters of the Gulf. From here the beach stretches 6.5 miles to the other end of the island. Paddle as much of this as you like, or go all the way to the end and return via St. Andrew Bay on the back side of the narrow island. Take out back at the boat ramp.

St. Joseph Peninsula State Park
St. Joseph Bay ◊ Gulf of Mexico

As its name suggests, the 2,500-acre park occupies a long, narrow strip of land. One of the many barrier land masses that shadow the Gulf coast, St. Joseph Peninsula branches off from the mainland at a right angle opposite the small city of Port St. Joe. It forms the barrier between the Gulf and St. Joseph Bay. The state park occupies most of the largely undeveloped finger of land. A campground, cabins, marina, and beach access are located near the park's southern end; the northern end is a wilderness preserve open only to hiking and primitive camping. For paddlers this offers the option for multi-day backcountry paddling trips on an exceptionally scenic part of the Gulf Coast.

Scenic that is, if you discount the vast paper plant in Port St. Joe that is something of an eyesore on the mainland coast. It's only visible from the bay side of the park, and there's plenty else to attract your gaze besides. Like the annual migration of hawks that turn the park into a mecca for birders each fall. The park is claimed to be the best place in the state to observe peregrine falcons. It's also on the list of best places to observe the annual migration of monarch butterflies, which pass through about the same time as the hawks. Of the more than 200 species of birds that have been counted at St. Josephs are herons, egrets, loons, grebes, gulls, terns, and the bald eagle.

Dense vegetation grows across much of the peninsula's interior. Here are found the sabal palms, pines, and live oaks of the pine-scrub habitat. Yaupon and wax myrtle form dense thickets that provide habitat for some of the mammals that inhabit these parts: fox, bobcat, raccoon, skunks, and an endangered species of beach mouse. White-tailed deer are commonly seen darting through the woodlands or foraging among the grasses. The dunes that rise behind the brilliant white sand beach that stretches the whole 14-mile length of the peninsula rise to a height of 60 feet, highest on the Gulf.

Most visitors who come to the park come seeking a natural refuge from the more crowded beach and resort communities that

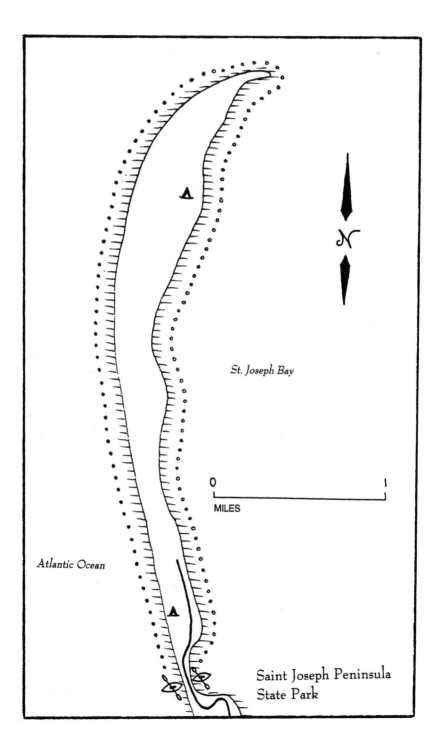

St. Joseph Bay

Atlantic Ocean

Saint Joseph Peninsula
State Park

N

line the coast all the way back to Pensacola. And they find it. Park amenities are few, but the opportunities for beach combing, swimming, fishing, or hiking are plentiful. The developed campground offers a convenient base for longer stays, as do the cluster of rental cabins.

With easy access to either the Gulf or St. Josephs Bay, kayakers can choose to paddle on either side of the peninsula. The choice is not an easy one. On the Gulf side is a 14-mile stretch of one of the most beautiful and deserted beaches in the United States. On the bay side is the wildlife-rich, intriguing world of an estuary and salt marsh. The best choice, undoubtedly, is to load your kayak with camping gear, spend a night in the backcountry wilderness, and paddle both.

INFORMATION: St. Joseph Peninsula State Park, Star Route 1, Box 200, Port St. Joe, FL 32456; 904/227-1327; www.dep.state.fl.us /parks/northwest/joseph.html. It costs $3.25/vehicle to enter the park. You can pick up maps, brochures, and camping permits at the fee station. Water and rest rooms are also available inside the park.

MAPS: NOAA 11393; USGS St. Joseph Point, St. Joseph Spit.

HAZARDS: The only real hazard in the area is other recreational boaters during the peak season. Tidal range: 1 foot.

BASE CAMP: Options for overnighting in the park include cabins, a 119-site car campground, and primitive backcountry camping at the northern end of the park. The wilderness sites are accessible by hiking or paddling. Permits are required and the sites cost $3/night. The developed car campground is open year round and sites cost $8–15/night depending on the season. Cabins cost $55–70/night.

PUT-IN: Access to both the Gulf and St. Joseph Bay is available in the park. From downtown St. Joe, drive S on US-98 2 miles to CO-30A (L it's 12.5 miles to US-98, R, and then 7.8 miles to downtown

Apalachicola). Turn R and go 6.6 miles to Cape San Blas Rd. Turn R and go 8.6 miles to the park entrance. Boat access is 0.9 miles further up the road.

DAY TRIP: *Sun, Sand, Sea. This trip follows the gentle arc of the peninsula's gulf shore for whatever distance you feel like paddling. The beach itself measures 16 miles from St. Joseph Point to Cape San Blas. Difficulty rating: 2.*

Put in at the beach access across from the marina. You'll have to portage across a boardwalk and the beach from the parking area, a distance of maybe 100 yards. Once you're on the water follow the coastline north. The white-sand beach runs about 8 miles up to St. Joseph Point. Along the way you're unlikely to see much except for shore birds, dolphins, and sea, sand, and sky. Paddle as far as you like, and when you're ready to return, retrace your route back to the put-in.

WEEKENDER: *St. Joseph Peninsula Circuit. This 16-mile route follows the curve of the peninsula first on the bay side and then on the Gulf of Mexico. Highlights are a chance to observe a variety of natural habitats, the long sandy beach, and a night spent in a remote part of the park. Difficulty rating: 3.*

Put in on the bay at the marina. Turn N and paddle along the peninsula's coast, which curves back toward the mainland in a gentle arc for 7 miles to St. Joseph Point. You'll have to make camp somewhere S of the point, as camping isn't permitted on the Gulf side beach. Once you've got camp set up, you can explore the natural habitats on the primitive road (closed to vehicles) that runs the length of the peninsula. On day 2 paddle out around the point and follow the Gulf beach S. You'll probably want to stop somewhere along the beach and get out and swim or just walk along the miles of empty sand. At 7 miles S of the point you reach one of the park beach accesses and a short boardwalk to the marina parking lot.

St. Vincent National Wildlife Refuge
St. Vincent Sound ◊ Gulf of Mexico ◊ Apalachicola Bay

A single barrier island and a small rectangle of land on the mainland comprise St. Vincent National Wildlife Refuge. The 12,300-acre island is distinct from the rest of those that line Florida's Gulf Coast, in that it lacks the familiar long, skinny profile. St. Vincent Island is roughly triangular in shape, bulging to four miles across at its widest point. The uninhabited, undeveloped island, unconnected to the mainland, can only be reached by boat. It's located just down the road from Apalachicola, a pretty little town that boasts a historic downtown district and a row of riverside restaurants that serve up the famed Apalachicola Bay oysters and other local seafood catches. In this quiet corner of the Gulf Coast, commercial fishing is the number one industry: 90% of Florida's oysters are harvested from these rich tidal waters.

Paddlers who visit St. Vincent will find an empty beach that stretches the full length of the island, and behind it, a wilderness oasis that supports white-tailed deer and red wolves, in addition to the flocks of brown pelicans and gulls that gather on the soft, white sands. Just offshore, dolphin are a common sight, their dorsal fins and sleek backs breaking the usually calm surface of the Gulf or bay.

Since no one lives on St. Vincent Island and you can only reach it by boat, it's just about deserted on most days. Which makes it a perfect destination for kayakers looking for an empty stretch of beach or wanting to explore the natural habitats of a barrier island. A network of sandy roads that criss-cross the island's interior facilitate the latter. You'll find pine forests, dunes anchored by sea oats, shrub thickets, and salt marsh spreading out into the bay. You can't camp on the refuge, since it's only open during daylight hours, but if you paddle past its eastern end you can set up camp on the Little St. George Island Preserve. Getting to the refuge couldn't be easier, since there's a boat ramp on the mainland only about a quarter mile away from the island's western tip.

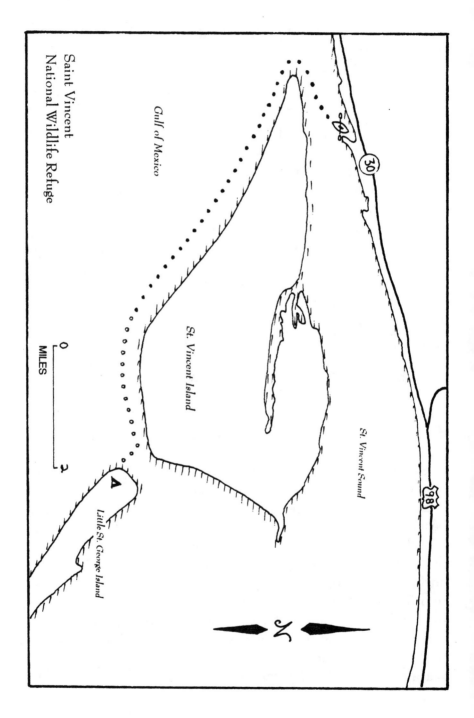

Saint Vincent
National Wildlife Refuge

Gulf of Mexico

MILES

0

2

St. Vincent Island

Little St. George Island

St. Vincent Sound

30

98

INFORMATION: St. Vincent National Wildlife Refuge, P.O. Box 447, Apalachicola, FL 32329; 904/653-8808; www.gorp.com/gorp/resource/us_nwr/fl_st_vi.htm. The refuge office is located on Market St. in Apalachicola (follow the signs). It's open weekdays from 8 am to 4:30 pm. You can pick up refuge maps and other info inside. An information kiosk with maps is located at the boat ramp.

MAPS: NOAA 11402, USGS Indian Pass, West Pass, (Cape St. George).

HAZARDS: The current in the channel at the put-in and behind the island is swift when the tide is coming in or going out. Commercial fishing boats are a presence in the area, but usually only in small numbers. Tidal range: 1 foot.-

BASE CAMP: Camping on the refuge is not permitted. You can, however, camp on uninhabited Little St. George Island, located at the eastern end of St. Vincent. Contact the Apalachicola Bay Estuarine Research Reserve (850/653-8063) for information and permits. The nearest car-accessible public campground is at St. Joseph Peninsula State Park. There are several hotels and B&Bs in Apalachicola. A favorite is the Gibson Inn, right in the heart of the town. It features wide, wrap-around verandas, unique rooms, and an outstanding restaurant and bar.

PUT-IN: From downtown Apalachicola, turn W onto US-98 and go 7.8 miles to SR-30. Turn L and go 9.7 miles to SR-30B. Turn L and go 2.9 miles to the boat ramp.

DAY TRIP: *Gulf Island Exploration. An unstructured paddle that follows the sandy shoreline of St. Vincent Island, with time out for exploring the refuge's interior on foot. Difficulty rating: 2.*
From the put-in, paddle S across the narrow channel known as Indian Pass. As you round the western tip of St. Vincent Island and turn SE, the long stretch of pristine beach comes into view. You can follow the shoreline for as many as 8 miles, where the

island curves around to front Apalachicola Bay. Ambitious paddlers may want to attempt a circumnavigation of the island, a total distance of about 22 miles. However far you plan to paddle, be sure to leave at least some time to wander the island's sand roads and explore the protected natural habitats on foot.

WEEKENDER: *St. Vincent to Little St. George. This 17-mile round-trip follows the Gulf shoreline of St. Vincent Island to the western end of uninhabited Little St. George Island, a component of the vast Apalachicola Estuarine Research Reserve. Difficulty rating: 3.*

From the put-in, paddle across narrow Indian Pass to the western end of St. Vincent Island. Turn S and paddle out around to the long, sandy beach that fronts the Gulf of Mexico. From here, follow the shoreline SE for 7 miles and then E for 2 miles to a narrow channel that separates St. Vincent from Little St. George Island. Camping is permitted at the western end of the island. 3.5 miles SE of there is the Cape St. George Lighthouse, a local landmark. On day 2 you can either retrace your route back to the put-in or follow St. Vincent Island around to the bay and sound side. This latter route is longer, about 13 miles in all.

St. George Island State Park
St. George Sound ◊ Gulf of Mexico

Like Gulf Islands National Seashore and St. Joseph Peninsula State Park, St. George Island is home to one of the finest beaches in Florida. Once you cross the toll bridge to the barrier island and drive past the long line of vacation homes and condominiums, you come to the park entrance and the start of a long, empty beach of fine white sand that stretches 9 miles to the island's eastern end. The beach is wide, flat, and slopes only gradually to the usually calm, turquoise waters of the Gulf of Mexico. Paddlers will be tempted to carry their kayaks across one of the boardwalks that provides beach access and spend the day cruising up and down the seemingly endless stretch of sand and sea, with maybe just a dolphin or two for company.

Another option is to begin a trip on the back side of the narrow island on Apalachicola Bay, where there are a couple of boat ramps and a primitive camping area that is only accessible on foot or by boat. Unfortunately, its location just a half mile from the boat ramp is less than ideal for weekend paddling trips, but if you want to avoid the usual crowds at the car campground it's not a bad choice. Whichever side of the island you choose to paddle, head for the remote eastern end, out past the end of the park road and beyond the reach of the beachgoing crowds. Across a 2-mile channel is Dog Island, an even more remote location with no bridge connection to the mainland.

Habitats at St. George are those common to the Gulf's barrier islands: beach, dunes, pine and hardwood hammocks, shrub thickets, and marsh. The wildlife is similar too. Bald eagles inhabit the park year round, and during the fall migration, the park is one of the best spots on the coast to view hawks, peregrine falcons, and kestrels. On the bay side, great blue herons, tricolored herons, and great and snowy egrets are often spotted. Endangered loggerhead sea turtles come ashore to nest on the beach during the summer months.

Swimming, sunning, and beachcombing are the most popular activities in the park, especially during the peak summer season.

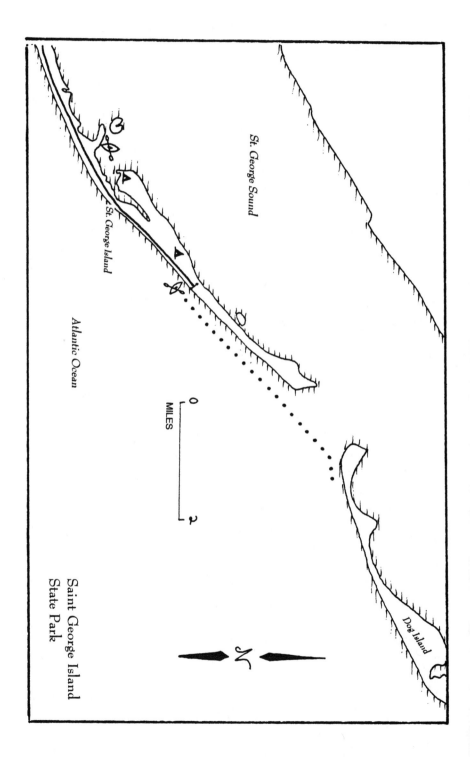

St. George Sound

St. George Island

Atlantic Ocean

MILES

0

2

Saint George Island
State Park

Dog Island

N

The developed car campground offers a convenient base for explorations further afield on this part of the coast. Fishing is another popular activity, both from the Gulf beach and in boats on Apalachicola Bay. While there are more remote places to paddle along the northern Gulf Coast, St. George's easy access makes it a good choice for a quick visit.

INFORMATION: St. George Island State Park, HCR Box 62, Eastpoint, FL 32328; 904/927-2111; www.dep.state.fl.parks/bigbend /stgeorge.html. Park maps, brochures, and camping permits are available at the entrance station. Water and rest rooms are in the park too. The park entrance fee is $2 for 1 person, $4 for 2–8.

MAPS: NOAA 11404, USGS Goose Island, Sugar Hill, Carrabelle.

HAZARDS: Boat traffic in the area includes anglers, sailboats, and other pleasure craft, though their numbers are usually relatively small. Tidal range: 1 foot.

BASE CAMP: The park has a developed campground and a primitive camping area that can only be reached by boat or on foot. Both are open year round. Sites cost $10/night in the developed campground, $3/night in the primitive area. The primitive site is completely undeveloped with no facilities.

PUT-IN: From downtown Apalachicola, turn E onto US-98 and go 5.8 miles to FL-300. Turn R and go 5.4 miles to East Gulf Beach Dr. Turn L and go 4.3 miles to the park entrance. There are a couple of boat ramps on East Cove. You can also put in on the Gulf side of the island, but a portage across the wide beach is necessary.

DAY TRIP: *Barrier Island Hopper. The 11.5-mile route of this trip takes you along the wide sand beach at the eastern end of St. George Island and across East Pass to Dog Island. Difficulty rating: 3.*
Put-in at the last beach access on the Gulf side of the island. Follow the long, empty sand beach NE for 3.5 miles to the end of St. George Island. Paddle across East Pass to the western end of

Dog Island, a distance of just under 2 miles. Dog Island is not connected to the mainland by a bridge, so you'll probably have the long sandy beach to yourself. You can paddle as much of the 7-mile shoreline as you like, or duck around and explore the island's sound side. When you're ready to return, recross East Pass and paddle back down the beach to your starting point.

St. Marks National Wildlife Refuge
Apalachee Bay ◊ St. Marks River ◊ Wakulla River

Of all the natural areas along Florida's portion of the Gulf Coast, none surpasses St. Marks as a destination for a trip that combines kayak touring with wildlife observation, particularly birding. The 95,000-acre refuge is home or temporary resting place to more than 250 species of birds, including raptors, wading birds, waterfowl, shore birds, and song birds. The high number is the result of the wide range of habitats located within refuge boundaries. Salt and brackish marsh, fresh-water impoundments, hardwood swamps, and pine flatwoods are all represented.

The vast refuge, 32,000 acres of which are on Apalachee Bay, sprawls along the coast between the Ochlockonee and Aucilla rivers. Although a refuge road and short hiking trails permit access to some of the natural habitats near the refuge's center, the only way to explore most of the acreage is in a boat. Shallow inshore waters, fragile ecosystems, and the abundance of wary wildlife all combine to make a kayak an ideal vessel for exploratory trips. You can paddle in the shadows of the tall, golden grasses of the salt marsh, circle tiny islands in the bay, head out for open water on the Gulf, or paddle inland on one of the rivers that drains the Panhandle's interior.

St. Marks is one of the oldest national wildlife refuges in the United States. It was established in 1931 to protect habitat for birds on their winter migrations. Prior to that, the area had a long history of human settlement. Archaeologists have gathered evidence of Indians settled here that dates back more than 10,000 years. Among the Europeans who migrated to this part of the Florida coast, the Spanish were first. By the end of the seventeenth century they had constructed a fort and founded the town of St. Marks, on the river of the same name. The ruins of the fort can still be seen today. A more popular landmark is the St. Marks Lighthouse, located at the end of the refuge's main road. The lighthouse was erected in 1831 and has been in use ever since. Kayakers will find it useful as a landmark in a landscape that is otherwise flat.

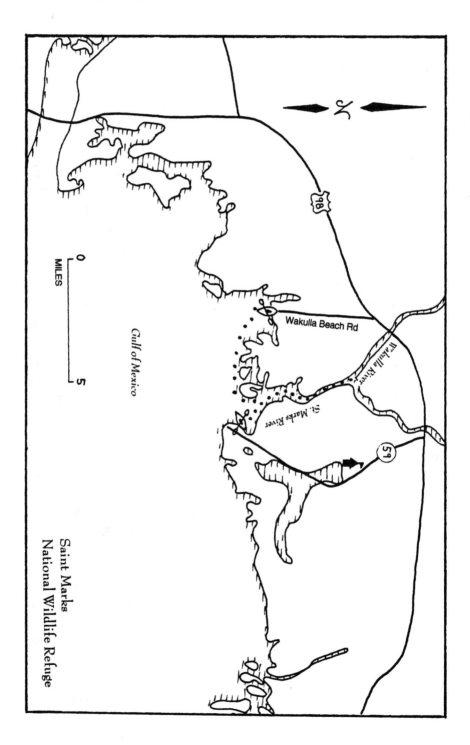

Although birds are the most abundant fauna on the refuge, they are by no means alone. A permanent population of more than 2,000 American alligators make the refuge their home. In the forested areas of the refuge are black bear, white-tailed deer, gopher tortoises, and wild turkeys. And bottle-nosed dolphin and river otters can sometimes be seen playing in the waters of the bay and rivers.

The refuge is only open daylight hours, so paddlers will have to be content to explore it in a series of day trips. You can get a pretty good sampling of the refuge's natural treasures in a single day, but a 2-day visit would give you the chance to linger and spend more time studying the astonishing variety of habitats and wildlife in this rich natural resource.

INFORMATION: St. Marks National Wildlife Refuge, P.O. Box 68, St. Marks, FL 32355; 904/925-6121; www.gorp.com/gorp/resource /us_nwr/fl_st_ma.htm. A $4/vehicle entrance fee is charged. An outstanding visitor center features exhibits and displays on the refuge's ecology. Maps and other info are available there, as are rest rooms and water. It's open weekdays from 8 am to 4:15 pm and weekends 10 am to 5 pm (closed federal holidays).

MAPS: NOAA 11405; USGS Sprague Island, Cobb Rocks, Spring Creek.

HAZARDS: Fishing and pleasure boats are a presence on the waters that surround the refuge, but their numbers are usually relatively small. Tidal range: 3 feet.

BASE CAMP: Camping is not permitted on refuge lands. The nearest public campground is at Ochlockonee River SP (904/962-2771). Sites cost $8–10/night and the campground is open all year.

PUT-IN: There's a boat ramp at the end of the refuge road. To get there: from US-98 20 miles S of Tallahassee, turn S onto SR-59. Drive 3.6 miles to the visitor center, 9.7 miles to the boat ramp.

TAKE-OUT: From the turn into the NWR on SR-59, drive W on US-98 5.9 miles to unpaved Wakulla Beach Rd. Turn L and go 3.8 miles to the end of the road where there's a boat ramp. 1.2 miles E of the turn is boat access to the Wakulla River.

DAY TRIP: *Gulf & River Wildlife Tour. This 20-mile route explores the diverse natural habitats native to the area. The chance to view avian and marine species of wildlife is outstanding. Difficulty rating: 3.*

Put in at the boat ramp at the end of the refuge road. Paddle out the short canal to the Gulf. Waterfowl, wading birds, and shore birds abound in the salt marshes and freshwater impoundments on this part of the refuge. Turn NNW and paddle toward the broad mouth of the St. Mark's River. Enter the river and paddle upstream 5 miles to Shell Island at the confluence with the Wakulla River. (A shorter version of this trip is possible by continuing up the Wakulla River for 3.5 miles to US-98, where there's a boat access). Turn around and paddle back out to the mouth of St. Marks River and past Sprague Island. Turn R and paddle W along the coast into Goose Creek Bay, about 2.5 miles away. The take-out is at the N end of the bay at the end of Wakulla Beach Rd.

Manatee Springs State Park
Suwannee River

This 2,075-acre park takes its name from one of the more than 40 springs that pump crystal clear water into the Suwannee River along its 235-mile journey from the Okefenokee Swamp in southeast Georgia to the Gulf of Mexico. The spring in turn was named after the large marine mammals that like to swim up the river from the Gulf in winter to take advantage of the warm water flowing from it. Each day nearly 117 million gallons of fresh water flow from Manatee Springs.

The state park has facilities for camping, hiking, mountain biking, and scuba diving. It is also a favorite starting point for boat trips on the magnificent Suwannee River. The storied river, made famous by Stephen Foster's song, is Florida's second largest. As it flows past the state park, its banks are crowded with a lush hardwood swamp forest. The stately bald cypresses draped with loose trellises of Spanish moss lend a haunting atmosphere to the scene, especially when fog hangs just above the river's surface.

The river's dark, slow-moving waters can be paddled in either direction. Along the way you will undoubtedly see some of the many wildlife species that make their homes along the river corridor. 100 different species of birds, including hawks, ospreys, and herons, inhabit the lower Suwannee. Alligators patrol the murky waters and sun themselves along the shore. Mammals such as white-tailed deer, coyotes, bobcats, foxes, and raccoons can sometimes be seen at the edge of the dense swamp forest.

From the park it's a 23-mile paddle to the river's mouth at the Gulf of Mexico. Several miles before that point the natural habitats change as the Suwannee's fresh water mixes with salt water pushed upriver by the tides. Swamp forest gives way to the golden prairies of salt and brackish marsh. The wildlife changes as well, with species adapted to saltwater habitats replacing those that can only survive in fresh water. Among the latter are the fish that inhabit the Suwannee above its estuarine section: largemouth bass, pickerel, crappie, and catfish. Their numbers are sufficient to make fishing a favorite activity on the Suwannee.

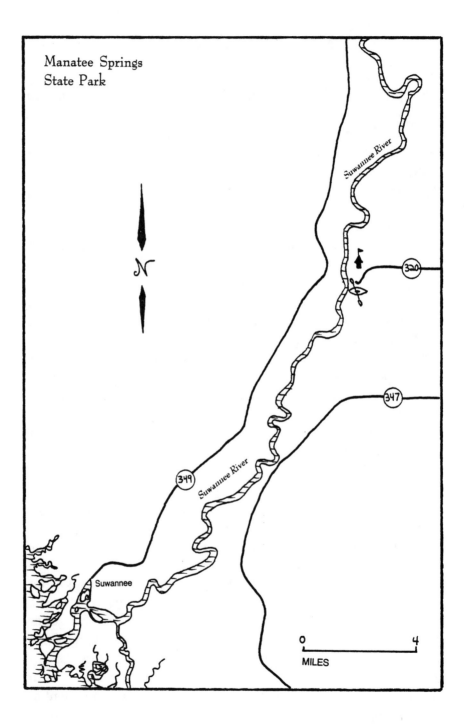

Manatee Springs
State Park

Suwannee River

320

347

349

Suwannee River

Suwannee

0   4
MILES

In recent years state agencies and the Nature Conservancy have joined forces to protect large sections of the Suwannee River's corridor. As you paddle up and down the river, you'll see few signs of civilization except for bridge crossings and the odd landing. You also won't see much in the way of facilities for extended trips. Don't let this deter you. The Suwannee is a favorite destination for long canoeing trips, and sea kayaks can negotiate most of the river equally as well. If you do plan to undertake a multi-day trip on the river, contact the park first to get a river map that shows boat ramps and locations suitable for primitive camping.

INFORMATION: Manatee Springs State Park, Route 2, Box 617, Chiefland, FL 32626; 352/493-6072; www.dep.state.fl.us/parks /northcentral/manatee.html. A $2/vehicle entrance fee is charged. Water, rest rooms, and pay phones are all located in the park. You can also pick up brochures, maps, and information about recent manatee sightings.

MAPS: USGS Manatee Springs, Fanning Springs, Vista, East Pass; NOAA 11408

HAZARDS: The Suwannee River is used by anglers and others piloting motor boats. Tidal range: 2 feet at the river's mouth; progressively less as you travel upriver.

BASE CAMP: The state park has a large, attractive car campground that makes an excellent base for trips on the Suwannee River. It's open all year and sites cost $10/night. Primitive backcountry camping is also permitted along the river. If you'd rather sleep in a bed, you can overnight at one of the few budget motels in Chiefland.

PUT-IN: A boat launch is located in the park. To get there: from US-19 in Chiefland, turn W onto FL-320. Go 5.7 miles to the park entrance.

TAKE-OUT: Same as the put-in. One-way trips are also possible, either upriver or down.

DAY TRIP: *Suwannee River Exploration. An unstructured paddle down Florida's most storied river. Highlights are the lush swamp forest and the wildlife it supports, as well as the possibility of seeing manatees. Difficulty rating: 2.*

Put in at the boat ramp in the state park. Paddle the short distance from the spring to the river. If manatees are in the area, odds are good that they are here, where the water temperatures are kept warm by the spring. When you reach the river, turn L and begin paddling downstream, where the river flows through a remote, uninhabited swamp forest. The odds of spotting many different wildlife species are good. The river flows for 23 miles through this pristine habitat before emptying into the Gulf of Mexico. However much of this you decide to cover, be sure to leave enough time to paddle back upstream to the state park, where you'll take out.

Cedar Keys National Wildlife Refuge
Gulf of Mexico

Of the many paddling destinations on Florida's Gulf Coast, none exceeds the Cedar Keys for their combination of a beautiful coastal setting and a charming, out-of-the-way fishing village. Here you can paddle the empty, aquamarine waters of the Gulf, stop for lunch on the sandy beach of a deserted island two miles out, and head back to town for a seafood dinner at sunset. Cedar Key and the surrounding islands are located just south of the Suwannee River delta, on one of the most remote stretches of the Gulf Coast. Only Cedar Key itself is inhabited: apart from vacation houses and rentals, the small village is home to a small artist's colony, a handful of hotels, and a row of modest seafood restaurants that perch above the brilliant blue waters that fade away to the distant horizon.

The wildlife refuge is comprised of the numerous small keys that dot the Gulf within a five mile radius of Cedar Key. Visitors have difficulty discerning just where the refuge's boundaries end, however, since virtually all of this part of the coast remains in a wild state. For kayakers, the refuge and surrounding waters offer an exceptional opportunity to tour a beautiful seascape where the monochromatic blues of sea and sky are interrupted with only splashes of green.

The islands and shallow tidal waters support one of the largest nesting populations of birds in Florida. As many as 50,000 birds inhabit the relatively small area at any given time. You won't doubt it as you paddle past the large flocks of brown pelicans that gather on the piers and abandoned buildings at Cedar Key. Other commonly seen species include great blue herons, anhingas, cormorants, egrets, gulls, and osprey.

Another species found here in surprising abundance is less welcome: cottonmouths, which inhabit the interior sections of Snake, Seahorse, and North keys. For this reason, and to protect fragile habitats, only the sandy beaches of the keys are open to visitors. Even so, the broad expanses of shallow water that surround the keys make it difficult to actually paddle all the way

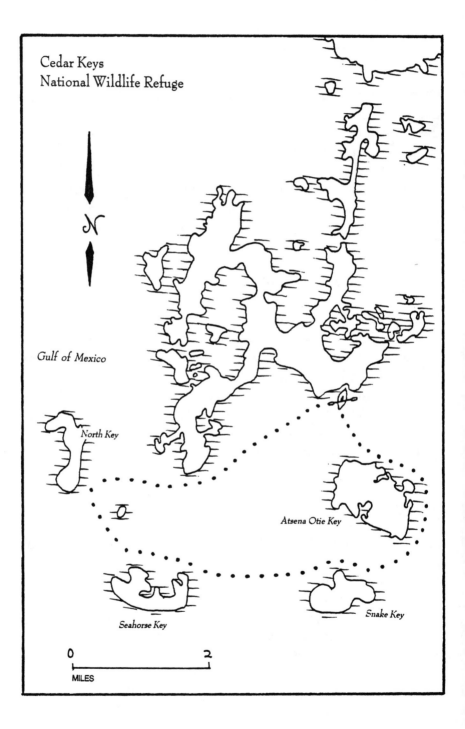

Cedar Keys
National Wildlife Refuge

N

Gulf of Mexico

North Key

Atsena Otie Key

Seahorse Key

Snake Key

0   2

MILES

to the beach in many places. You may have to get out and walk your kayak across the flats. There's plenty to see on the islands, with mangrove swamps, salt marsh, coastal shrub thickets, and upland forests. Colonies of fiddler crabs scuttle across the sands as you approach, and the ubiquitous birds usually stake out the spits of sand that rise a few inches above the water's surface. In deeper water, dolphins are often seen cruising offshore.

The islands of the refuge are only open during daylight hours, and camping isn't permitted. Still, you'll probably want to stay in this idyllic locale for at least a weekend, perhaps much longer. A handful of waterfront hotels make this possible; at some, you can practically launch your kayak from your front door.

INFORMATION: Cedar Keys National Wildlife Refuge, Route 1, Box 1193C, Chiefland, FL 32626; 904/493-0238; www.gorp.com /gorp/resource/us_nwr/fl_cedar.htm. There is no on-site source of information for the refuge. Water and rest rooms can be found in the town of Cedar Key.

MAPS: NOAA 11408; USGS Cedar Key, Seahorse Key.

HAZARDS: Commercial fishing vessels and pleasure boats ply the waters around the keys, but not in sufficient numbers to disturb the air of serenity that pervades this part of the Gulf. Tidal range: 2.5 feet.

BASE CAMP: Camping is not permitted on any of the keys. A small selection of B&Bs, hotels, and motels is available in Cedar Key. Contact the Chamber of Commerce at 904/543-5600 for information.

PUT-IN: From I-75 near Gainesville, take exit 75. Turn W onto FL-24 and go 51.6 mi to Second St in Cedar Key. Turn L and go 0.2 mile to a park and boat ramps, R.

TAKE-OUT: Same as the put-in.

DAY TRIP: *Cedar Keys Circuit. This 11-mile route begins at the charming Cedar Key waterfront and makes a loop that includes 4 of the largest offshore keys. Highlights are the spectacular scenery, remote location, and the abundance of wildlife. Difficulty rating: 2.*

Put in at the waterfront boat ramp and paddle out the inlet to the sheltered Gulf waters. Turn SE and paddle 0.5 mile to Atsena Otie Key. Follow the E side of the island and head S toward Snake Key, 1.5 miles away. Once you reach Snake Key, turn W and paddle 1.5 miles to Seahorse Key. You may want to land on the beach here and take a break for lunch or just explore the flats or sandy beach (the island's interior is closed to visitors). The next stop is North Key, 1.75 miles NNW. From there, it's a 3 miles paddle back to the Cedar Key waterfront and the boat ramp.

Crystal River National Wildlife Refuge

Crystal River ◊ Kings Bay ◊ Crystal Bay

Crystal River National Wildlife Refuge was created in 1983 to provide protected habitat for the large numbers of endangered West Indian manatees that gather here every winter. As the waters of the Gulf cool from December to March of each year, the large marine mammals swim up the Crystal River to its source, Crystal Springs. Water flows from the springs—more than 600 million gallons each day—at the constant temperature of 72°. With more than 200 manatees migrating here each winter, the refuge offers the best opportunity in Florida to be assured a chance to observe these popular animals. In fact, since the refuge is small—only 43 acres—and lacks the extensive natural habitats of most of the nation's other refuges, there really isn't any other reason to visit.

Crystal River NWR encompasses several small islands and protected underwater zones at the head of the Crystal River in the town of the same name. During winter no wake restriction are in effect to help protect the manatees from propeller scars. A kayak is an ideal boat for tracking the animals, since it presents less of a disturbance to the manatee's habitat than any other type of vessel. Paddlers may want to bring along snorkeling gear, since the refuge offers the only chance in Florida to actually swim with and observe the manatees under water. Be forewarned, however, that if you come on a winter weekend the bay will be filled with small boats ferrying snorkelers and divers to the manatees. A solitary wilderness experience it won't be.

After viewing the manatees in Kings Bay, paddlers may want to head out the Crystal River toward the Gulf of Mexico. Gradually the residential development that lines the shores of the bay and upper river give way to natural habitats. An exception is the nuclear power plant which looms at the mouth of the river and remains in constant view. As you paddle out the river, many of the other wildlife species that inhabit the area become apparent. Great blue herons wheel overhead, snow egrets track the river in an effortless glide, and anhingas, cormorants, white ibises, and

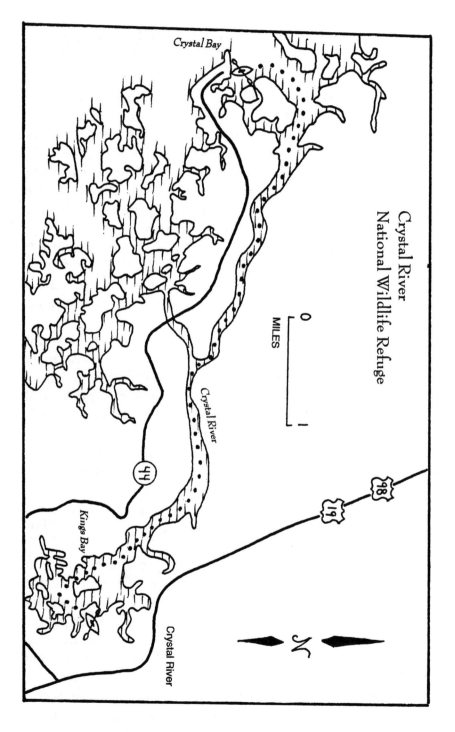

Crystal Bay

Crystal River
National Wildlife Refuge

MILES

0

1

Crystal River

44

Kings Bay

19

98

Crystal River

N

ospreys also soar through the sky. Beneath the water, tarpon, mullet, and largemouth bass challenge the skills of sport fishermen.

The refuge is only open during daylight hours, and camping isn't permitted, so if you want to stay for more than a day, you'll have to be content to make a series of day trips. In truth, you can cover all of the refuge and river in a single day. And, aside from the manatees, there are more appealing destinations for paddlers looking for wild Florida than the Crystal River.

INFORMATION: Crystal Springs NWR, 1502 S.E. Kings Bay Dr., Crystal River, FL 34429; 352/563-2088; www.gorp.com/re-source/us_nwr/fl_cryst.htm. You can pick up a refuge map and information about the manatees from the refuge office.

MAPS: NOAA 11409; USGS Crystal River, Red Level.

HAZARDS: The concentration of boats ferrying snorkelers and divers around the bay can get pretty thick. Further down the Crystal River beyond the no wake zone, pleasure and fishing boats are a concern. Tidal range: 2 feet at the mouth of the river.

BASE CAMP: Camping is not permitted on the refuge and there are no public campgrounds nearby. You'll find a handful of hotels and motels in Crystal River.

PUT-IN: Access is at Pete's Pier, a private marina. There's no charge to launch a kayak. To get there: from US-98 in downtown Crystal Springs, turn E onto SE Kings Bay Dr. Go 0.6 mi to Pete's Pier, R. The refuge HQ is another 0.8 miles up winding SE Kings Bay Dr.

TAKE-OUT: For day trip 1, take out at Pete's Pier. The take-out for day trip 2 is at the mouth of the Crystal River. To get there from US-98, turn W onto FL-44 and go 9 miles to the end of the road and a boat ramp.

DAY TRIP 1: *In Search of Manatees. This short paddle explores the islands and waterways of Kings Bay, where manatee sightings are common, especially during winter. Difficulty rating: 2.*

Put in at the boat ramp at Pete's Pier and paddle the short distance out into the bay. If there are manatees present, you can probably locate them by following the small flotilla of boats carrying scuba divers and snorkelers that seem inevitably to follow in their wake. Aside from the manatees, a variety of raptors, wading birds, waterfowl, and shore birds can usually be seen in the bay. In all, you probably won't paddle more than 2 or 3 miles, unless you head out the Crystal River toward the Gulf.

DAY TRIP 2: *Crystal River to Crystal Bay. A 7-mile one-way paddle from Kings Bay to the mouth of the Crystal River on the Gulf. Highlights are manatees in the bay and the vast expanses of salt marsh and uplands downriver. Difficulty rating: 2.*

Put in at the boat ramp at Pete's Pier. You may want to begin this trip by spending some time exploring Kings Bay, where the manatees gather areas that have been designated a wildlife sanctuary. From the bay, it's a little over six miles out to the mouth of Crystal River and the Gulf of Mexico. As you paddle downriver, the homes that line the banks gradually give way to natural habitats. The cooling tower of the nuclear power plant on Crystal Bay is an exception; it's visible for the entire trip. As you near the mouth of the river, take the L channel and follow it SW to the boat ramp at the end of FL-44.

Anclote Key State Preserve
Anclote River ◊ Anclote Anchorage ◊ Gulf of Mexico

Anclote Key is the northernmost of the 320-mile-long chain of islands that parallels the southwest Florida coast and helps shield it from the worst effects of Gulf storms. Like all barrier islands, Anclote is a work in progress, its size and shape constantly shifting with the forces of wind, weather, and tide. Unlike many of the other barrier islands, however, Anclote is also being altered by the geologic forces that first elevated it above the Gulf's surface. And this process is occurring with lightning speed, at least in geologic terms. Since 1957 the island has grown 30 percent in size, and the northern hook that curves back toward the mainland has only appeared in the last 20 years.

The narrow strip of land, located offshore from Tarpon Springs, stretches 4 miles from end to end. It is entirely uninhabited, though a lighthouse and a pair of keepers' houses on the southern end attest to its earlier role in providing navigation to seafarers. Today mariners rely on sophisticated electronic equipment for navigation, and kayakers will have no problem finding the island, which is in plain sight from the mainland, three miles to the east. Unconnected to the mainland by bridge or road, it is accessible only by boat.

Apart from Anclote Key's historic role, it is known primarily as a nature preserve that offers protection for the coastal habitats endemic to barrier islands and the wildlife they sustain. Visitors to the island will find sandy beaches, a small dune system, maritime forest, mangrove swamp, tidal marsh, and mesic flatwoods. Almost 50 species of birds are the most readily seen wildlife, including the endangered bald eagle. Dolphins are sometimes seen breaking the water's surface just offshore, and raccoons emerge from their woodland homes at dusk to scour the shore for a meal.

Visitors come to Anclote Key to escape the beach crowds so common to the nearby heavily developed coast. A handful of fishing boats might be plying the aquamarine waters just offshore, and sailboats sometimes moor overnight in the natural anchorage

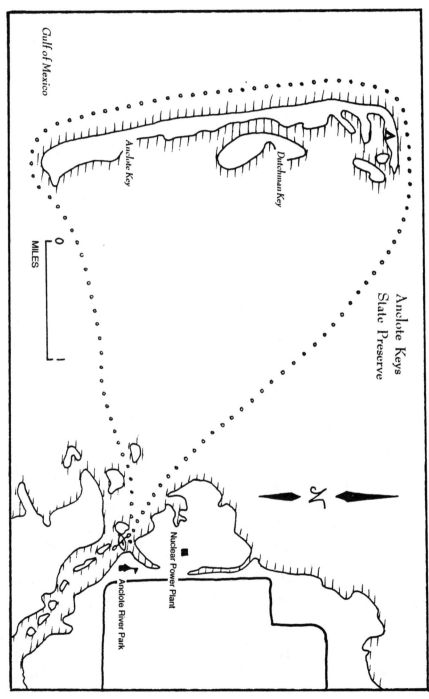

Gulf of Mexico

Anclote Key

Dutchman Key

Anclote Keys
State Preserve

MILES

0

Nuclear Power Plant

Anclote River Park

on the island's eastern side. The usually deserted beach of fine white sand on the island's Gulf side invites long walks and searches for seashells. Primitive camping is permitted on Anclote Key, though there are no facilities and no water. The island's small size and location just over an hour away from the mainland by kayak make it the ideal destination for a weekend retreat. Trips begin at the Anclote River Park, where there's a boat ramp, picnic facilities, water, and rest rooms.

INFORMATION: Anclote Key State Preserve, c/o Gulf Islands Geopark, #1 Causeway Blvd, Dunedin, FL 34698; 813/469-5942; www.dep.state.fl.us/parks/west/anclote.html. Brochures, maps, and other info are available from the Honeymoon Island SRA visitor center, located at the end of the Dunedin Causeway (FL-586), 2.6 miles from US-98 ALT. There are no facilities on Anclote Key.

MAPS: NOAA 11411; USGS Tarpon Springs.

HAZARDS: Boat traffic is relatively heavy in the area, particularly near the park and in the channel that leads out to Anclote Key. Tidal range: 3 feet.

BASE CAMP: Primitive camping is permitted on the northern end of Anclote Key. No fee or permit is required. On the mainland, there are no public campgrounds in the vicinity. Hotels and motels are available in Tarpon Springs and Holiday.

PUT-IN: Use the boat ramp or small beach in Anclote River Park. From US-98 ALT, turn W onto Anclote Blvd and drive 2 miles to Bailie's Bluff Rd. Turn R and go 0.2 miles to the park entrance, L. If you're going to leave your vehicle overnight in the park, a permit ($5) is required, available at the Holiday Rec Center. Leave the park and go N on Bailie's Bluff Rd 2.2 miles to Old Stauber Hwy. Turn R and go 0.5 mile to the rec center, R.

TAKE-OUT: Same as the put-in.

DAY TRIP/WEEKENDER: *Anclote Key Exploration. This route runs between the mainland and the 3.5-mile-long island. Out and back is an 8-mile trip. If you add a circumnavigation of the island it's about 12 miles. Difficulty rating: 3.*

Put-in at the boat ramp or on the sandy beach at Anclote River Park. Follow the main river channel out to the open waters of the Gulf, about a mile away. From there, head WNW and paddle 2 miles out to the N end of Anclote Key. You can spend time exploring the uninhabited coastline or find a place to make camp. On day 2 you might want to paddle out around to the front of the island and head down to the S end where the lighthouse is located. When you're ready to return to the mainland paddle E and keep the large power station to your left as you enter the Anclote River.

Cayo Costa State Park
Boca Grande ◊ Gulf of Mexico

1,200-acre Cayo Costa State Park occupies most of Lacosta Island, one of the string of barrier islands that shelters Florida's Gulf Coast from the brunt of tropical storms. The 7-mile island separates the Gulf from Charlotte Harbor and Pine Island Sound. No bridge connects the island to the mainland, so the only way to arrive is by boat. Commercial ferry services bring visitors to the island from several points on surrounding islands and the mainland, and there's a dock on the island's sound side for private boats. Visitors come to stroll along the miles of empty beach, swim in the clear gulf waters, fish from shore, or camp in the very attractive park campground. The park also operates a cluster of small cabins that are both popular and inexpensive ways to spend more than just a day on the island.

The shortest route for paddling trips to Cayo Costa is from the Gasparilla State Recreation Area just across Boca Grande channel. This is a good place to pick up a map of the park or get any other information you might need, since there's no park office or visitor center on Cayo Costa itself. You can fill up on water too, though running water is available in the park campground on the island. The first part of the trip is the most treacherous, since it involves crossing the channel, where currents can reach 8–9 knots at the peak of ebb or flood tide. Try to cross during a slack tide, and exercise extra caution.

Once you reach the island, the paddling is some of the most enjoyable on the southwestern Florida coast. A long, sandy beach runs the length of the island on the Gulf side, offering the chance to land just about anywhere. Behind the beach, palmettos, live oaks, and pines crowd together in a lush subtropical forest that offers a cool retreat from the often glaring sun. The park campground is set at the edge of the forest where it opens out onto the beach. On the island's sound side, a swamp forest of dense mangroves grows at the lower elevations.

Both the Gulf and sound sides of Cayo Costa attract a diversity of wildlife. Avian species are the most abundant, with brown

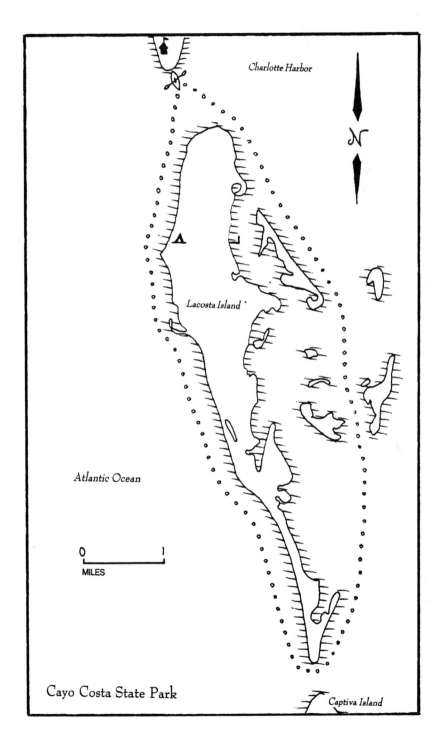

Charlotte Harbor

N

Lacosta Island

Atlantic Ocean

0   1
MILES

Cayo Costa State Park

Captiva Island

pelicans, herons, egrets, plovers, terns, and gulls all fairly common. Gopher tortoises make their burrows on the island, and small mammals such as raccoons become active at dusk.

INFORMATION: Barrier Islands GEO Park, P.O. Box 1150, Boca Grande, FL 33921; 941/964-0375; www.dep.state.fl.us/parks /southwest/cayo.html. On-site information about the park is available at the Gasparilla SRA. You'll also find water and rest rooms there.

MAPS: NOAA 11427; USGS Captiva.

HAZARDS: Currents in the Boca Grande Pass reach 8–9 knots during maximum ebb or flood tide. Only strong paddlers should attempt to cross it. The channel is also a fairly busy boating lane. Tidal range: 2 feet.

BASE CAMP: On Cayo Costa you have a choice of cabins or an adjacent campground. The area is very attractive and there are rest rooms with running water. Cabins cost $20/night, campsites $13/night.

PUT-IN: Access is from the Gasparilla SRA. From I-75 take exit 35. Turn S onto Jarracunda Blvd and go 5.2 miles to FL-776. Turn L and go 8.6 miles to Placida Rd. Turn R and go 8.8 miles to Gasparilla Rd. Turn R and go 5.8 miles to 5th St. Turn R and go 0.1 mile to Gulf Blvd. Turn L and go 2.2 miles to the end of the road and the SRA entrance.

DAY TRIP/WEEKENDER: *Cayo Costa Exploration. This paddle begins and ends at the southern tip of Gasparilla Island. A short version takes you out and back to the campground at Cayo Costa SP, a distance of 4 miles. A longer version circumnavigates the island, for a trip distance of 15 miles. Difficulty rating: 5.*

Put-in at the sand beach next to the lighthouse on Gasparilla Island. It's best to time your crossing of Boca Grande to coincide with slack tide. Paddle S across the channel to the N end of

Lacosta Island, a distance of about 0.75 miles. Follow the island's gulf coast S for just over a mile to a large brown SP sign on a beach that fronts the camping and cabin area. Land about 100 yds S of the sign. From there, the island extends S 5 miles to Captiva Pass. Depending on when you arrive on the island, you can explore as much of this as you like.

On day 2, you can either spend time exploring the island on foot and then return to Gasparilla SRA, or begin a circumnavigation of the island. If choosing the latter, follow the island's coastline SSE for 4 miles to Captiva Pass. Turn E and paddle through the short channel and then turn NNW and begin following the island's sound side. The ICW passes about a mile offshore, but you can paddle between the island and the smaller keys that are closer in. As you head N the island widens and the shoreline is irregular. After 7 miles you'll reach the N end of the island. Turn WNW and cross Boca Grande to the launch site at Gasparilla SRA.

The Everglades
& Florida Keys

Everglades & Florida Keys Key Map

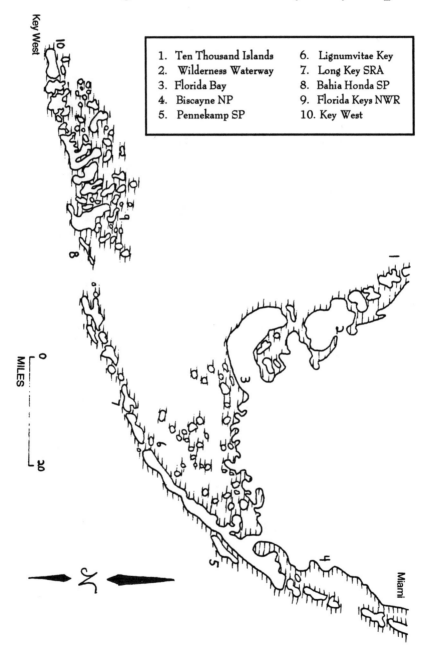

1. Ten Thousand Islands
2. Wilderness Waterway
3. Florida Bay
4. Biscayne NP
5. Pennekamp SP
6. Lignumvitae Key
7. Long Key SRA
8. Bahia Honda SP
9. Florida Keys NWR
10. Key West

Key West

MILES
0
20

N

Miami

Weather Readings at Key West, FL

Month	Air Temp (High F°)	Water Temp F°	Wind Speed (mph)	Wind Direction
January	75°	69°	12	NE
February	75°	70°	12	NE
March	79°	75°	12.5	NE
April	82°	79°	12	NE
May	85°	83°	10.5	ESE
June	88°	86°	10	ESE
July	89°	87°	9.5	ESE
August	89°	87°	9	ESE
September	88°	86°	10	ESE
October	84°	82°	11.5	ESE
November	80°	76°	12.5	ESE
December	76°	72°	11	ESE

Everglades National Park
Gulf of Mexico ◊ Florida Bay ◊ Wilderness Waterway

The Everglades is one of those increasingly rare places whose importance and appeal are almost impossible to exaggerate. With boundaries that encompass more than 1.5 million acres of sawgrass prairie, mangrove swamps, pine and hardwood hammocks, and the turquoise waters of Florida Bay, Everglades National Park is the largest wilderness area east of the Mississippi River. It also represents an ecosystem that occurs nowhere else on the planet. In recognition of its uniqueness and central role in the functioning of south Florida's ecosystems, the park has been designated a United Nations World Heritage Site and an International Biosphere Reserve.

All is not well with the Everglades, however. The seasonal flow of a broad sheet of water—what Marjory Stoneman Douglas called a "river of grass"—from Lake Okeechobee to Florida Bay is essential to the delicate balance of natural habitats here. In the past half century, that balance has been disturbed, distorted, and in many ways broken, as the natural course of the water has been diverted to serve the needs of agriculture and exploding human populations. As a result, the Everglades is not receiving the lifeblood it needs to survive. A 90% drop in the population of wading birds is just one of the symptoms of this desiccation. In recent years, conservation groups and, belatedly, the state and federal government, have begun the massive project of restoring the Everglades to a state that at least approximates a sustainable equilibrium.

Visitors to the Everglades cannot mistake its essential wildness. For one thing, much of it is inaccessible. The vast interior, a sun-drenched plain of saw grass interrupted only here and there by small pockets of forested uplands, is a wetland where water and land are in a constant state of flux. Although the habitat sustains a wide variety of flora and fauna, its lack of firm ground or defined waterways makes it ill-suited to humans. The climate is inhospitable as well. Summers are intensely hot and humid, and the million-acre basin of fresh water is the perfect breeding ground for mosquitos, whose abundance from May to November keeps most visitors at bay. Peak season for park visitors is during the dry season from December to April, when temperatures are comfortable and the mosquitos less intense.

Despite its degradation over the past fifty years, the Everglades' diverse habitats still host a wide range of flora and fauna. More than 900 species of plants and 600 species of marine and terrestrial animals have been identified. Included among these are endangered species such as the wood stork, snail kite, manatee, American crocodile, and Florida panther, which numbers fewer than 30 animals in the wild. More commonly seen fauna are dolphins, alligators, herons, egrets, anhingas, brown pelicans, white pelicans, roseate spoonbills, and ibises.

Although short hiking trails provide access to a few select areas of the Everglades, by far the best way to explore this vast wetland is in a boat. Powerboats are permitted just about everywhere in the park, but only the shallow draft and natural stealth of a kayak (or canoe) will permit you to explore the many natural habitats unobtrusively. A kayak seems to be made for negotiating the maze-like waterways of the Ten Thousand Islands, paddling beneath overhanging limbs on narrow waterways, or island-hopping in Florida Bay. A handful of canoe trails offer a chance to explore some of the Everglades' inland habitats, but it's the immense estuary of bay and gulf and the 99-mile Wilderness Waterway that seduce most paddlers. Where else in the continental United States can you paddle through a wilderness for a week or two and never retrace your route?

All of the paddling trips described in the following sections begin at either of two visitor centers: Gulf Coast in Everglades City or Flamingo. Day trips will give you a taste of the Everglades' allure, but with more than 41 backcountry campsites spread out within a day's paddle of one another, the opportunity to spend at least one night under the stars shouldn't be passed up. There are three types of sites: beach sites on gulf and bay islands, land sites in small clearings, and chickee sites on 10 x 12 elevated platforms. Most sites have vault toilets, some have picnic tables, none have water. Extended backcountry paddling trips should not be undertaken lightly; the harsh conditions and lack of facilities require careful planning and a readiness to alter plans.

INFORMATION: Everglades National Park, 40001 State Road 9336, Homestead, FL 33034-6733; 305/242-7700; www.nps.gov/ever. Park visitor centers are located W of Homestead (the main visitor center), in Everglades City, and at Flamingo. Maps, park information, and backcountry camping permits are available at each. Rest rooms and water are also at the sites.

MAPS: Listed below under each of the individual headings.

HAZARDS: Boat traffic is fairly common along most of the paddling routes in the park, but particularly on the Wilderness Waterway. The typical hazards encountered kayaking in south Florida—relentless sun, mosquitoes, unpredictable and often violent weather—are only intensified by the Everglades' remoteness.

BASE CAMP: One of the main appeals of the Everglades for backcountry explorers is the opportunity to spend up to a week or two in remote wilderness. A $10 permit is required to camp at any of the 41 backcountry sites. There are also three developed car campgrounds in the park. Additional information is given below under each of the separate areas.

PUT-IN/TAKE-OUT: Described below under each of the separate areas.

Ten Thousand Islands

There aren't really ten thousand of them, of course. But it can certainly seem that way as you paddle around the curve of one mangrove island to what you think will be open water, only to be faced with another wall of green and a handful of possible routes into blind passageways. The exact number of islands here in the northwest corner of Everglades National Park is moot, anyway.

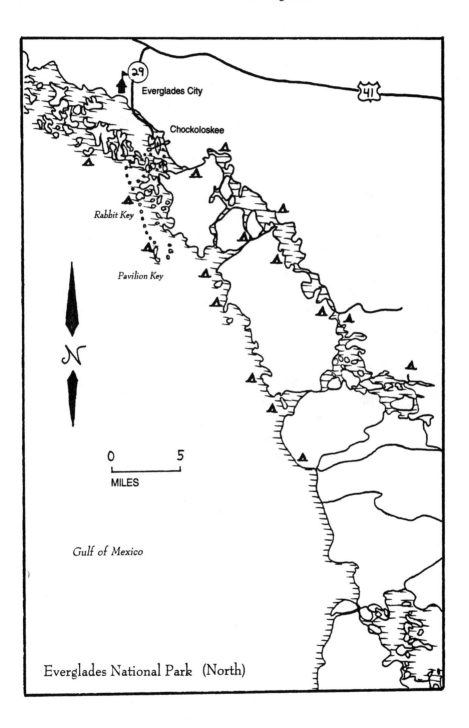

Everglades National Park (North)

Islands are constantly being created and destroyed by the natural rhythms of this vast estuary. Mangroves reproduce by casting cigar-shaped seeds onto the water to be carried on the tides to a shallow landing. There roots emerge and anchor themselves in the sandy bottom. As the trees grow quickly their root system expands, trapping dirt and other floating detritus. Gradually enough material accumulates to form a small island. If the island survives long enough it might reach several hundred acres in size. Eventually a violent storm strikes, as Hurricane Andrew did in 1992, and the mangrove island is destroyed.

Seen from above, the islands appear like so many green gems scattered carelessly across an aquamarine velvet background. In a kayak, a nautical chart is essential to have even a chance of navigating through the labyrinthine waterways that wind among the islands. Local fishermen know these waters by heart, but odds are good that your only encounters will be with the wading birds and shore birds that stalk the shallow waters for prey or maybe with a manatee or dolphin. Since the only way to explore the islands is by boat, this is one of the lesser visited corners of the park. It is also the northern terminus of the Wilderness Waterway, and paddling routes that combine the Ten Thousand Islands with the waterway further inland are popular. Give yourself at least a long weekend to get away from the main boat channels and disappear into the remoter reaches of this subtropical wonderland.

INFORMATION: Water, rest rooms, and a pay phone are available at the Gulf Islands Visitor Center. If you're going to camp in the backcountry, be sure to pick up a permit before heading out. Nautical charts—for sale on the premises—are absolutely essential for paddling the unmarked waterways of this corner of the park.

MAPS: NOAA 11430; USGS Chockoloskee, Everglades City, Pavilion Key, Plover Key, Lostmans River Ranger Station.

HAZARDS: Power boats share the waterways that wind through the islands with canoeists and kayakers, but their numbers aren't usually great. Tidal range: 3 feet.

BASE CAMP: There are 9 primitive backcountry camping areas on the Gulf between Everglades City and the mouth of Lostmans River. The sites are primitive, with vault toilets but no water sources. The required $10 backcountry camping permit is available at the Gulf Islands Visitor Center.

No public campgrounds are located on the mainland part of the park here. There are a couple of private campgrounds in Everglades City, as well as a handful of hotels and motels.

PUT-IN: From the jct of US-41 and FL-29, turn S onto FL-29 and go 4.6 miles to the park entrance and visitor center, R. The boat ramp is located 2.7 miles further down FL-29 on the L just before the Outdoor Resorts compound.

TAKE-OUT: Same as the put-in.

DAY TRIP: *Rabbit Key Run. This 12-mile loop meanders among dozens of the islands that dot this part of the park. Highlights are an abundance of wildlife and a lack of motorized boat traffic. Difficulty rating: 3.*

From the put-in at Chockoloskee, follow the curve of the island S past boat slips and a couple of marinas. Turn SW and begin following the twisting path of Chockoloskee Pass. The route is marked with wooden stakes, but you'll still need a nautical chart and compass to avoid wrong turns and blind alleys. After 3 miles you reach the open waters of the Gulf. Turn S to SSE and head for Rabbit Key, the outermost island. It's 3 miles away. Once there you can get out and explore some of the key on foot, or paddle around some of the other islands in the area. When you're ready to return, paddle NNE just over a mile to Turtle Key. Paddle around the outside of the key and turn NE into Rabbit Key Pass, a relatively straight course back to Chockoloskee Bay. Once you reach the bay, it's about 2 miles back to the boat ramp.

WEEKENDER: *Gulf Island Overnight. This 20-mile round-trip explores the various natural habitats encountered in this part of the everglades.*

The campsite is on the exposed beach of Pavilion Key. Difficulty rating: 3.

Follow the route described above under "daytrip" to Rabbit Key. From there it's a 4-mile paddle SSE across open water to Pavilion Key and the camping area. The island is fronted by a narrow, sandy beach, which curves around and extends for part of the back side as well. The only facility on Pavilion Key is a pit toilet. On day 2, paddle back to Rabbit Key and then follow the second half of the daytrip route back to the boat ramp on Chockoloskee.

EXPEDITION: *Gulf Coast Exploration. An unstructured 3–10-day trip into the backcountry of the northwest corner of Everglades NP. The opportunity to explore the largest, remotest wilderness in the Southeast is reason enough for the trip. Difficulty rating: 4.*

Paddlers wanting to spend more than a night or two in the backcountry have several options. One is a one-way trip from Chockoloskee to Flamingo, a distance of 69 miles. 12 campsites line the route, although the trip can be paddled in about a week. Another option is a round-trip that keeps to the Gulf islands. The 9 campsites between Everglades City and the mouth of Lostmans River offer numerous route options. A final option is to create a loop that combines paddling among the Gulf islands with a return trip via the Wilderness Waterway. A 3-day version of this trip would use the Chatham River as the connector. A 6- or 7-day trip would run S to Lostmans River and then back up the Wilderness Waterway.

Wilderness Waterway

The 99-mile Wilderness Waterway is one of the premier canoe and kayak trails in the nation. Following a winding route across bays, rivers, and the Gulf of Mexico, the trail provides access to the interior of one of the wildest regions in the nation. The definition of this vast backcountry as a wilderness is a matter of some contention, however: unlike most wildernesses, motorized boats are permitted along the entire length of the trail. There's no denying that the whine of engines and the boats' wakes diminishes the backcountry experience for canoeists and kayakers. Fortunately, however, the waterway is so tight in some places and so shallow in others that only very small boats with shallow drafts can negotiate the trail's entire length. While this may be small consolation for wilderness purists, it does eliminate the possibility of large, speeding powerboats barreling down on unsuspecting kayakers.

The Wilderness Waterway offers kayakers the best means to experience most of the major natural habitats that comprise the Everglades. Along the route you'll paddle through maze-like corridors among mangrove islands, across brackish and salt water, and past pockets of coastal prairie and pine and hardwood hammocks. Wildlife is abundant, and a highlight of any day's paddle. Crocodiles patrol the inland waters, dolphins and manatees break the surface of Gulf waters, and dozens of species of wading birds, shore birds, and raptors can be seen overhead, stalking the flats, or just hanging out on the mangroves' leafy limbs.

Small sections at the northern or southern end of the Wilderness Waterway can be explored during a day's paddle, but most kayakers and canoeists choose to spend at least a weekend, and often a week or more, on the trail. If you plan on paddling the route from one end to the other, give yourself at least a week. Such a trip should not be undertaken lightly or without considerable advance planning. With the right conditions, the Everglades can seem like a subtropical paradise. But in a region as wild and unforgiving as this one, adventurers unprepared for the unexpected or for simply harsh conditions—unrelenting sun, sudden storms, stiff winds, and swarms of mosquitos—will certainly come to regret it.

INFORMATION: The waterway runs between 2 visitor centers, Gulf Islands in Everglades City and Flamingo on Florida Bay. Information, maps, and camping permits are available at either. Rest rooms and water are also at both locations.

MAPS: NOAA 11430, 11432, 11433; USGS Everglades City, Chockoloskee, Pavilion Key, Alligator Bay, Lostmans River Ranger Station, Big Lostmans Bay, Harney River, Shark Point, Whitewater Bay West, Whitewater Bay East, Flamingo, Lake Ingraham West.

HAZARDS: This is the part of the Everglades with the most motorized boat traffic, although the number of boaters is still relatively small. Tidal range: 1–2 feet.

BASE CAMP: 22 primitive backcountry campsites line the Wilderness Waterway. Some are right on the main route, others require a paddle of 1–5 miles on secondary waterways to reach. A $10 backcountry camping permit is required before heading out. Pick one up at the Gulf Coast or Flamingo visitor centers. Sites must be reserved in advance, but no more than 24 hours before your time of departure.

A developed car campground is located next to the Flamingo Visitor Center at the S end of the Wilderness Waterway. Sites cost $14/night.

PUT-IN: Boat ramps are at both ends of the waterway. Directions to the ramp at Chockoloskee are under the previous section; and to the ramp at Flamingo in the next section.

TAKE-OUT: Use the same boat ramps under put-in.

WEEKENDER 1: *Northern Waterway Weekend. This 30-mile trip takes you south from Chockoloskee across open bay and through a pair of narrow, winding rivers. Overnight is at the Watson Place, the site of a former homeplace. Difficulty rating: 3.*

Put in at the boat ramp at Chockoloskee. Paddle SSE across Chockoloskee Bay 3 miles to the mouth of the Lopez River. Turn ENE into the river and paddle 2 miles to marker #126 at the entrance to Crooked Creek, R. Paddle into and up the creek to marker #125, less than a mile away. Turn R and paddle in a SE direction across Sunday Bay, Oyster Bay, and Huston Bay. After 5 miles you reach marker #107. Turn R and paddle down an arm of the Chatham River to the main channel, a little over 2 miles away. Turn R and paddle less than half a mile to the campsite, on river R. The sites are in a large elevated clearing beside the river. A couple of picnic tables and a port-a-toilet are at the site. On day 2, retrace your route back to the put-in at Chockoloskee.

WEEKENDER 2: *Bay & River Exploration. A 23-mile round-trip route through the Buttonwood Canal, Coot Bay, and the St. Joe River. The campsite is on a chickee at the edge of a coastal prairie. Difficulty rating: 3.*

Put in at the boat ramp in Flamingo. Paddle N up the Buttonwood Canal to Coot Bay, 3 miles away. Turn NNW and paddle 2 miles across the bay and through Tarpon Creek to the more open water of Whitewater Bay. Turn W and follow the shoreline for 6 miles to a channel of the St. Joe River. The chickee is on the banks of a small embayment. On day 2 retrace your route back to the boat ramp at Flamingo.

EXPEDITION: *Wilderness Waterway End to End. A 96-mile paddle that runs almost the entire length of one of the nation's most famous boat trails. After a week in the Everglades backcountry, you'll have an understanding and appreciation for this wilderness much deeper than those who stay for only a day or two. Difficulty rating: 4.*

You can paddle this trip from either end, putting in at the boat ramp at either Chockoloskee or Flamingo. Although strong paddlers in a rush could cover the trail in 4 days (under ideal weather conditions), give yourself 7–10 days. Along the way you have 22 backcountry campsites to choose from, some right on the waterway, others 1–5 miles off the main route. Plan your trip well in advance and make sure you carry enough water to last the entire time.

Florida Bay

Paddle the shallow, aquamarine waters of Florida Bay and you might see a brightly plumed roseate spoonbill searching the flats for a meal. Or the bulging eyes and scaly back of a crocodile patrolling the waters. Or the dorsal fin and smooth skin of a dolphin as it arcs above the water's surface. You'll certainly see wading birds such as great blue herons, snowy egrets, and white ibises. Out on the bay you can circle the small islands where mangroves form an impenetrable thicket. Or paddle to a backcountry campsite as the sun sinks below the flat horizon of the Gulf of Mexico. Ambitious paddlers might want to island-hop all the way across the bay to the keys, a 3-day journey one way.

Florida Bay stretches from the southern tip of the mainland peninsula to the Florida Keys. In between, the brilliantly hued water is bespeckled with small clusters of green—the mangrove islands that accent an otherwise featureless landscape of sea and sky. Flamingo is the headquarters for this part of the park, and though this is the area that receives the highest concentration of visitors, only a small percentage venture out onto the bay. That's unfortunate, since the only way to really experience this vast estuary is in a boat. With depths that rarely exceed six feet and are often less than two, a kayak is the ideal vessel for exploring this part of the Everglades backcountry. A couple of backcountry campsites on tiny keys make it possible to overnight in the park's remotest locales.

In addition to the open waters of the bay, most of the park's canoe trails are here, as is the southern end of the Wilderness Waterway. There are more facilities here too than elsewhere in the park, with a visitor center, marina, lodge, and campground all at Flamingo.

INFORMATION: The Ernest Coe Visitor Center, located just before the park entrance and pay station, is open daily from 8 am to 5 pm. Inside are exhibits, a bookstore, and water and rest rooms. At the end of the road is the Flamingo Visitor Center, open daily from 9 am to 5 pm. Water and rest rooms are also available here. The Key

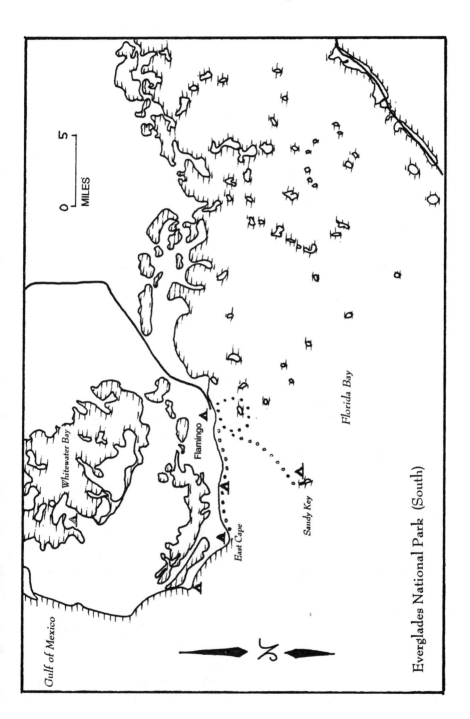

Everglades National Park (South)

Largo visitor center, open seasonally, is located on US-1 at MM 98.7. A $10 entrance fee and $3 boat surcharge are required at the park's main entrance. Both fees are valid for 7 days.

MAPS: NOAA 11433, 11452; USGS Flamingo, Clive Key, Sandy Key, West Lake, Pelican Keys.

HAZARDS: Fishing boats and other motorized craft are a presence on the bay. Concentrations are highest near the marina at Flamingo. Tidal range: 2 feet.

BASE CAMP: Backcountry camping is permitted on 3 of the keys in Florida Bay, at sites along the Gulf Coast mainland, and on the Wilderness Waterway. A $10 permit, available at the Flamingo Visitor Center, is required. There's also a developed campground (rest rooms, showers, drinking water) at Flamingo. Sites cost $14/night.

PUT-IN: From the jct of US-1 and Palm Dr. in Homestead, turn W onto Palm Dr. and go 1.6 miles to FL-9336. Turn L and go 7 miles to the park entrance. 0.5 mile further ahead is the main park visitor center. It's another 37 miles to the Flamingo Visitor Center and boat ramp. Use the boat ramp furthest to the right between the visitor center and marina.

TAKE-OUT: Same as the put-in.

DAY TRIP: *Prairie, Bay, Keys. This 10-mile loop follows the Everglades' southern coast before heading out to the open water of Florida Bay and an exploration of a handful of keys that rise from its shallow waters. Difficulty rating: 2.*

From the put-in next to the Flamingo Visitor Center paddle out to the bay and turn W. Follow the coast for 3 miles to tiny Curry Key. Turn S and paddle 2 miles to Oyster Keys, a pair of islands next to the larger Murray Key. Paddle E across the shallows—depths average a foot—to Catfish Key and Frank Key. At Frank Key turn N and head back to the visitor center and boat ramp, 2.5

miles away.

WEEKENDER 1: *To the Edge of the World. A 24-mile circuit across the open waters of Florida Bay. Overnight is on Carl Ross Key, located at the edge of the park and the last island before the vast expanse of the Gulf of Mexico. Difficulty rating: 3.*

From the boat ramp, paddle S past Murray Key (2.5 miles) and reach Clive Key at 4.5 miles. Turn WSW and paddle 4 miles to a channel through the First National Bank (it may be possible to paddle over the bank if the tide is in). Paddle through the channel and turn S. The N end of the island is less than a mile away.

On day 2 paddle S from the island and then turn E, following the S edge of the First National Bank to Man of War Key, 6 miles away. Turn N and paddle past Johnson Key (1 mile) to Clive Key, 3 miles away. Continue N, paddling between Murray Key and Frank Key, to the Flamingo area and boat ramp, 4 miles distant.

WEEKENDER 2: *Destination: East Cape. A 20-mile round trip that traces the southern edge of the Florida mainland. Overnight is at a beach campsite where the Gulf of Mexico and Florida Bay meet. Difficulty rating: 2.*

Put in at the boat ramp next to the Flamingo. Visitor Center Paddle W and follow the coastline past Bradley Key (1.75 miles), Curry Key (3 miles), and the Clubhouse Beach campsite (8 miles) to East Cape, 10 miles from the put-in. The campsite there is on the beach and affords spectacular views of the Gulf and Florida Bay. On day 2, retrace your route back to the boat ramp at Flamingo.

Biscayne National Park
Biscayne Bay ◊ Atlantic Ocean

Created in 1980, this large park sprawls across 181,500 acres of bay, key, and ocean south of Miami. Unique among national parks, 96% of Biscayne is under water. The park preserves four primary natural habitats, each dependent on the other: mangrove-rimmed mainland, bay, key, and ocean. A stunning variety of marine and terrestrial wildlife depends on the bounty offered by these habitats for sustenance.

In Biscayne Bay sea beds anchor a sandy bottom just six to twelve feet below the surface. The blue-green waters are astonishingly clear, and the bottom is easily visible from a kayak crossing the bay. Manatees favor the warm-water habitat, as do dolphins and dozens of species of birds and fish. Starfish, sponges, crabs, and other bottom-dwellers feed off the rich soup of plankton provided by the light and warmth of the sun. Brown pelicans cruise the water's surface, then rise and suddenly dive once they've zeroed in on a fish swimming near the surface. Wading birds too use the bay as a hunting ground, stalking their pray in the ankle-deep flats at the edge of the mangroves.

The narrow stretch of mainland shoreline included in the park is grown over with mangrove swamps in the longest stretch of this important wetland habitat in the nation. The mangroves not only maintain the purity of Biscayne Bay's water, but provide a nursery for dozens of fish species as well. The presence of fish inevitably attracts birds; they can often be seen perched on the trees' canopies or searching the waters near the maze-like roots for a meal.

Biscayne's keys are the northernmost links in the long chain of islands that stretches southwest for 150 miles to Loggerhead Key in the Dry Tortugas. They were formed from ancient coral beds that were exposed when sea levels dropped. If you land your kayak on one of the keys, you can see the fossilized coral at the water's edge. On higher land, a lush sub-tropical hardwood forest reigns. Dense hammocks of gumbo limbo, mahogany, strangler fig, and Jamaican dogwood, to name just a few of the species,

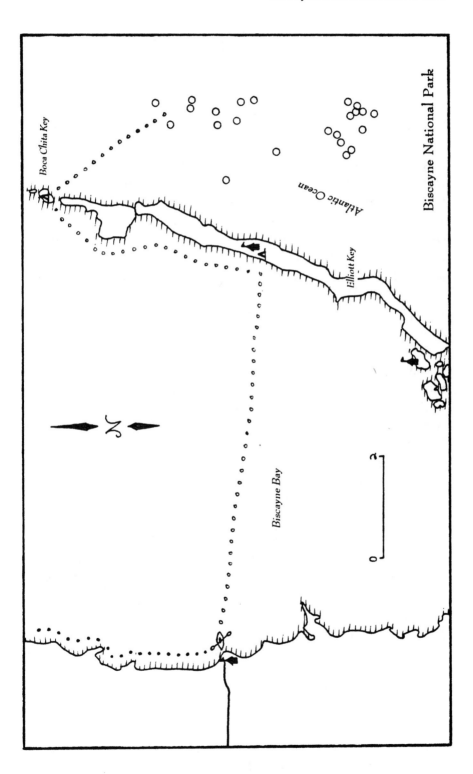

create a green world rioting with life. One species native to this habitat that you won't appreciate is the mosquito; they're as fierce here as anywhere on the Florida coast.

Of the many reasons to visit Biscayne, perhaps the most compelling is the underwater paradise of the coral reefs found just beyond the keys on their Atlantic side. Here the duotone of sea and sky is replaced by colors so vivid and lifeforms so varied that it seems they must belong to some other world. The corals themselves provide the architecture for these exuberant underwater cities. Varieties such as brain, elkhorn, finger, and star coral are formed from the limestone secretions of millions of tiny animals called polyps. Living among the corals are the hundreds of species of tropical fish that bring the underwater realm to life. So astounding are the brilliant colors, wild patterns, unexpected forms, and sheer beauty of this exotic environment that even the most vivid landscapes of the terrestrial world seem bland in comparison.

There's no better way to discover the different worlds of Biscayne National Park than in a kayak. You can explore parts of the park in a day or two, but to really have time to appreciate is varied environments you should give yourself at least three. Especially if you plan on snorkeling at the reefs. They're located at least ten miles from the mainland boat ramp, so you'll have to set up a base at one of the camping areas on the keys. For those without snorkeling gear or enough time, glass-bottom boat tours of the reefs are run from the visitor center.

INFORMATION: Biscayne National Park, P.O. Box 1369, Homestead, FL 33090-1369; 305/230-7275; www.nps.gov/bisc. Begin your trip at the Convoy Point Visitor Center. Inside you can pick up maps and brochures, check on current conditions and weather forecasts, view a 15-minute film about the park, or get a camping permit. Rest rooms, water, and a pay phone are also at the site. The entrance is open from 8 am to sundown.

MAPS: NOAA 11463, USGS Arsenicker Keys, Elliott Key.

HAZARDS: Power boats and other water craft are a presence throughout the park. Be particularly careful crossing the channel at Convoy Point. Tidal range: 2.5 feet.

BASE CAMP: The best way to get a real feel for the park's natural environments is to set up camp on either Elliott Key or Boca Chita Key. Both camping areas are accessible only by boats, which keeps the number of campers to a minimum. Elliott Key has rest rooms with showers and running water; Boca Chita Key is primitive. Camping is free, but a permit is required. On the mainland, the closest lodging is at several budget motels that line US-1 in Homestead.

PUT-IN: From the jct of US-1 and Lucy St, turn E onto Lucy St and go 8 mi to the entrance, L. There's a small launching area beside the headquarters. ◊ Or, from US-1 turn E on Palm Dr and go 6 mi to Six Mile Rd. Turn L and go 1 mi to North Canal Dr. Turn R and go 2 miles to the entrance, L.

TAKE-OUT: Same as the put-in.

DAY TRIP: *Mainland Mangroves. This unstructured paddle along the mainland shoreline allows an opportunity to explore mangrove habitats and the shallow bottom of the bay. Difficulty rating: 2.*
    Unless you're looking for an extreme workout, an out-and-back trip to Biscayne's keys isn't really possible in a single day. Instead you can paddle up or down the extensive mainland shoreline, which harbors the longest intact stretch of mangrove swamps in the country. Your best bet is to paddle N, away from the large nuclear power station just S of the visitor center. The park boundary extends more than 10 miles, more than enough coast to cover in a single day. And you'll probably want to spend some of the time exploring the intimate confines of the narrow creeks that cut through the mangroves. The put-in is at the sandy landing next to the visitor center.

WEEKENDER: *Biscayne Bay Exploration. This 18-mile round-trip consists primarily of an open-water crossing of Biscayne Bay. The 9-mile trip should leave plenty of time to explore the coast of Elliott Key or explore its center on foot. Difficulty rating: 5.*

From the put-in it's a straight shot across Biscayne Bay to the camping area on Elliott Key. Head about 10° S of due E, making sure to compensate for tides or prevailing winds, which can be stiff. From the put-in your destination is barely visible to the naked eye, so you might want to bring a small pair of binoculars. Use the 2 tan-roofed buildings—the visitor center and bathhouse at the campground—as landmarks. Make camp and watch the sun set over the bay and mainland. On day 2, retrace your route back to the NP headquarters. In this direction, the nuclear power plant just S of the launch site serves as an all-too-visible landmark.

EXPEDITION: *Bay, Keys, Coral Reef. This 31-mile, 3-day trip offers a chance to explore all of the park's various habitats. After a paddle across Biscayne Bay, 2 nights are spent on the keys, with one day devoted to snorkeling in the coral reefs. Difficulty rating: 5.*

Put in next to the visitor center and follow the directions above to Elliott Key. From there, turn NNE and follow the line of the keys 5 miles to Boca Chita Key, where you'll make camp. On day 2 paddle to the ocean side of the island and turn SSE. 3 miles away is a tower and mooring buoy above Bache Shoal. You can tie up at the buoy or anchor in the shallows nearby. Several patch reefs are in the vicinity (be sure to pick up a park map before you start this trip). At the end of the day, turn around and paddle back to Boca Chita Key. On day 3 you can either paddle straight across the bay back to the visitor center (10.5 miles), or follow the line of keys S 5 miles, stopping at Elliott Key for lunch. From there, it's a 9-mile paddle back across Biscayne Bay.

John Pennekamp Coral Reef State Park
Largo Sound ◊ Atlantic Ocean

The nation's first underwater park, Pennekamp State Park encompasses 70 square miles of Atlantic coast and a large part of the United States' only living coral reef. Of the park's 56,000 acres, all but 2,350 on Key Largo are submerged. As you look out across the ocean from the park mainland, all you see is an endless expanse of sea and sky. And although the shadings of sky blue and aquamarine can themselves dazzle, the unbroken horizon is flat and featureless. Just beneath the water's surface, however, the world explodes in a vivid display of color, movement, and form.

The park is one of the busiest in Florida, and crowds are common. Because of the fragility of park environments, only a fixed number of visitors are permitted in the park; once that level is reached, the gates are closed. Facilities inside the park include a large campground, a nature trail, canoe trail, small swimming beach, glass-bottom boat and snorkeling tours, marina, and dive concession. The park was named in honor of the *Miami Herald* editor who championed the creation of Everglades National Park and fought for protection of what would later become Pennekamp State Park.

Habitats on land are primarily mangrove swamps and subtropical hammocks. Offshore, the reefs are built of 45 different types of coral and teem with more than 600 species of fish, many of them brilliantly colored. The corals fall into two main categories: stony corals and octocorals. Stony corals, such as brain, elkhorn, and star, are formed from the limestone skeletons that the living corals secrete, while octocorals, such as sea fans, are flexible and sway with the ocean current.

Most visitors to the park come to see the coral formations and the amazingly diverse marine life they support. Scuba diving, snorkeling, and glass-bottomed boat trips are all popular ways to explore the undersea wonderland. For kayakers, the reefs offer an opportunity for a paddling trip unlike any other in the United States, and a challenge as well. Since the reefs are located between 3 and 5 miles offshore, kayakers must first paddle across the open

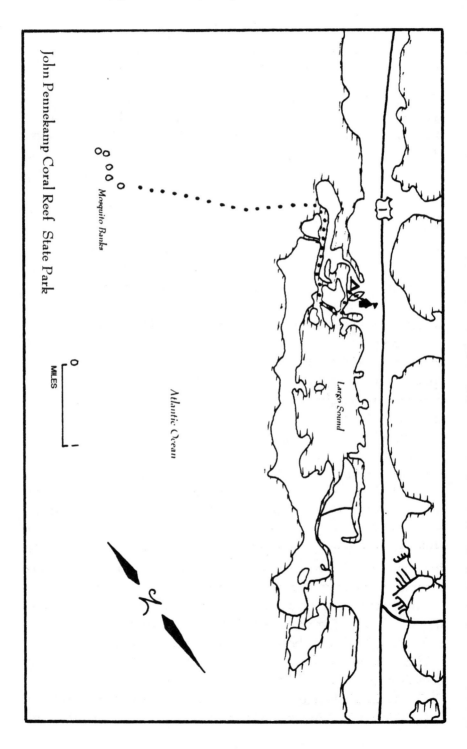

John Pennekamp Coral Reef State Park

Mosquito Banks

Atlantic Ocean

Largo Sound

MILES

0

1

I

ocean to reach them. Fortunately the waters here are usually quite serene, with the reefs themselves acting as the buffers that eliminate the wave action of most ocean shores. Since most paddlers will want to don snorkeling gear and explore the reefs up close, exiting and then reentering the kayak far from land is necessary. For most paddlers, this is much easier in an open-deck kayak than in a touring, closed-deck model. Once paddlers reach the reefs, they can tie on to one of the mooring buoys designed for that purpose. The waters are shallow enough to drop anchor in most places, but anchoring above the reefs themselves is strictly prohibited.

INFORMATION: John Pennekamp Coral Reef State Park, P.O. Box 1560, Key Largo, FL 33037; 305/451-1202; www.dep.state.fl.us /parks/south/pennekamp.html. The park entrance fee is $2.50. The heavily developed park has a large visitor center and concessions for diving, canoeing, and eating. Check in at the dive center before launching for maps and information about paddling out to the coral reefs.

MAPS: NOAA 11451, USGS Rock Harbor.

HAZARDS: The popularity of the park as a base for trips out to the coral reefs makes the waterways here some of the busiest on the keys. Paddlers should be prepared to share the water with numerous power boats and other pleasure craft. Tidal range: 2.5 feet.

BASE CAMP: A developed campground is located in the park. Reservations are accepted (and are recommended from December to April) by phone or in person up to 60 days in advance. The sites cost $19/night and the campground is open year round. Other lodging options are available in Key Largo.

PUT-IN: The park entrance is on the ocean side of US-1 at MM 102.8. Use the boat ramp next to the dive center.

TAKE-OUT: Same as the put-in.

DAY TRIP: *Coral Reef Exploration. A 10-mile round-trip paddle to Mosquito Banks, 3 miles offshore in the Florida Straits. The main highlight is the chance to explore the unique world of the coral reefs, so be sure to bring snorkeling gear. Difficulty rating: 4.*

From the boat ramp, paddle out the marked narrow channel to its entrance 2 miles away. With all the motorboat traffic, paddling this channel can be something of an anxiety-inducing experience. Where the channel meets open water, turn ESE and paddle to the red triangular #2 daymarker, 1 mile away. Turn S and paddle 1.75 miles to a tower that marks Mosquito Banks. On very calm days the reef is visible from above the surface. If you're planning on snorkeling, tie up to one of the 6 mooring buoys at the reef and display a diver down flag. When you've finished exploring the area, retrace your route back to the boat ramp in the park.

Lignumvitae State Botanical Site
Florida Bay ◊ Atlantic Ocean

280-acre Lignumvitae Key preserves the best remaining example of a habitat that was once common to the upper keys—the tropical hardwood forest. Here grow dense hammocks of tropical tree species at the northern edge of their range: gumbo-limbo, Jamaica dogwood, strangler fig, mastic, poisonwood, black ironwood and lignum vitae. Unlike just about everywhere else on the keys, the forest here has never been logged. Park naturalists estimate that some lignum vitae trees on the island are at least 1,500 years old and have a natural lifespan of four or five thousand years. This helps explain the tree's name, which is Latin for "tree of life." In addition to its unsurpassed longevity, another unusual feature of the lignum vitae is the extreme density of its wood, which weighs an astonishing 75 lbs per cubic foot. The wood of the black ironwood, also found here, is even heavier, weighing 85–90 lbs per cubic foot.

Once you reach the island by kayak, you're free to get out and explore the exotic world of the tropical forest, but with a couple of catches. First, you're not allowed to roam about the island yourself, but must take one of the ranger-led tours. This restriction is to limit the number of visitors at any one time and thereby protect the island's fragile environment. A couple of other precautions: the poisonwood tree is so named because it has the same effect on skin as poison ivy. And mosquitoes on the island are abundant and fierce; bring repellent and wear long sleeves and pants. The tours leave from the Matheson House, Thursday to Monday at 10 am and 2 pm. The house was built in 1919 by William Matheson, one of the island's owners. It's next to the dock and beach landing.

A mile south of Lignumvitae Key is Indian Key, a solitary 10-acre gem that rises from the vast blue-green emptiness of sea and sky. A state historic site, this tiny island was briefly the setting for a string of events that included shady business dealings, deft political maneuvering, and an Indian attack that ended in murder and arson. At the center of the swirl of events was Jacob

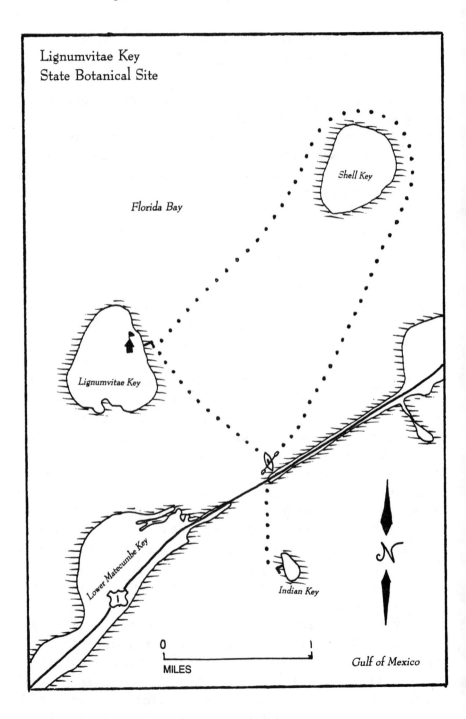

Lignumvitae Key
State Botanical Site

Housman, who purchased the island in 1831. He was one of the many salvagers who made a fortune capitalizing on ships that sank on the treacherous reefs of the Florida Straits. Troubles in Key West, the capital of the salvage business, led him to establish Indian Key as the center of his own salvage empire. To further insulate himself from Key West, he had his island made the seat of newly-formed Dade County in 1836. His fortunes waned, however, and all of the island's buildings were burned, and some of the residents killed, by the Seminoles during an attack in 1840. Today, the layout of the town and the ruins of the Houseman house can be seen on the uninhabited island. Ranger-led tours leave from the dock at 9 am and 1 pm Thursday through Monday.

Both Lignumvitae and Indian keys are the remnants of coral reefs that lived when the ocean here was 20–30 feet higher. The region surrounding the islands is predominantly covered by shallow sea grass beds, and, in deeper waters, small coral reefs. Both marine habitats are fragile and require care on the part of paddlers not to cause undue damage.

INFORMATION: Lignumvitae Key State Botanical Site, P.O. Box 1052, Islamorada, FL 33036; 305/664-4815; www.dep.state.fl.us/parks /south/lignumvitae.html. On the island, information is available at the visitor center in the Matheson House, from which all walking tours of the island leave.

MAPS: NOAA 11463; USGS Upper Matecumbe Key.

HAZARDS: Fishing boats and other pleasure craft are common in this part of the keys, particularly around Islamorada, which bills itself as the "Sport-Fishing Capital of the World." Tidal range: 2.5 feet.

BASE CAMP: Camping is not permitted on any of the keys featured in the trip below. The nearest public campground is at Long Key SRA, about 9 miles W (see separate entry below). The closest backcountry campsite is on Rabbit Key, 12 miles offshore in Florida Bay and a part of Everglades NP. For hotels, resorts, and other lodging in the area, contact the Islamorada Chamber of Commerce at 800/322-5397.

PUT-IN: A boat launch and parking area are located at the E end of the bridge across Indian Key Channel at MM 79 on US-1.

TAKE-OUT: Same as the put-in.

DAY TRIP: *Indian Key, Lignumvitae Key, Shell Key. A 7-mile circuit around 3 keys located just off the mainland. Highlights are historical settlements, tropical forests, and marine life in the crystal-clear shallows. Difficulty rating: 2.*

From the roadside put-in off of US-1, paddle NW toward the E side of Lignumvitae Key. After a little more than a mile you reach a dock and a sandy area for landing canoes and kayaks just S of it. If you're taking the walking tour of the island, check in at the house that serves as the preserve's HQ. After you've finished exploring the island, paddle 2 miles ENE to Shell Key. You can't get out and explore the key's interior, but you can paddle around its perimeter and study some of the flora and fauna of a mangrove key. As you come around to the S end of the key, turn SSW and paddle back toward the highway, 2 miles away. As you pass under the bridge, head for Indian Key, less than a mile away on the Ocean side of the Keys. You can land here next to the dock and get out and explore the islands and the ruins of the former settlement. When you're ready to return, paddle the short distance back to the put-in on US-1.

Long Key State Recreation Area
Zane Grey Creek ◊ Long Key Bight ◊ Atlantic Ocean

Cayo Vivora, the Cayusa Indians called it, Rattlesnake Key, for its resemblance to the open jaws of a snake poised to strike. Its current, less colorful name, refers to its shape as well, though it ignores the lower "jaw" of the snake. Located about midway down the keys, Long Key makes a good base for explorations further afield. About half of the key is occupied by the 965-acre recreation area; most of the rest is primitive as well, with dense mangroves and lush subtropical forest covering the majority of the acreage. Park attractions include an oceanside campground, two nature trails and an observation tower, canoe trail, and picnic area.

Long Key is most popular with swimmers and sunbathers, who stake out a patch of the half-mile sandy beach. The shallow water stretches way out into the ocean, inviting wading, but making it necessary for kayakers to walk their vessels at least part of the way if they plan on landing on the beach. The other main attraction is the subtropical forest and the wildlife that it and the park's other natural habitats nurture. Caribbean and West Indian tree species—gumbo limbo, mahogany, Jamaica dogwood, and poisonwood—crowd together in dense hammocks. The most visible wildlife are the wading birds that frequent the key's shallow edges. Egrets and herons are especially abundant. Dolphins are sometimes seen too, and if you bring snorkeling gear, you can explore the underwater realm just offshore. In fact, Long Key is the remnant of a coral reef left over from a time when the sea level was considerably higher than it is now.

Human history on Long Key dates back to the Cayusa Indians, who were the first to settle the island. After the Spanish began to colonize Florida in the sixteenth century, the Indians were eventually pushed out. During the next several centuries Europeans made their way to the keys from various surrounding islands, but it wasn't until the early twentieth century that the string of islands became easily accessible. It was then that Henry Flagler built the railroad that extended from the mainland to Key

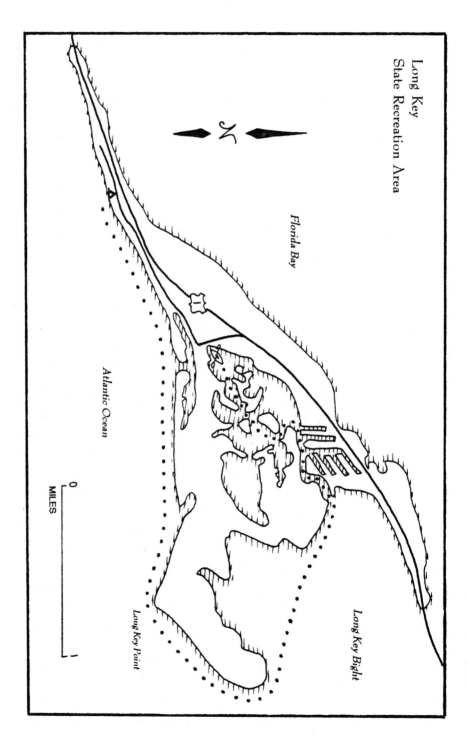

Long Key
State Recreation Area

Florida Bay

Atlantic Ocean

Long Key Bight

Long Key Point

MILES

0

1

West. Hundreds died in the endeavor, but it put Long Key on the map. The island became an important stop along the route and home to the Long Key Fishing Club, a gathering place for the world's elite saltwater anglers. A devastating hurricane in 1935 made short work of both Flagler's railroad and the fishing club. Although the fishing club was not rebuilt, the rail line was eventually sold to the state of Florida and became the foundation for US-1. Florida also acquired much of the land on Long Key, and in 1969 the park was established.

With a canoe trail that winds through a maze of mangrove hammocks and the clear, aquamarine waters of the ocean, there's enough to explore around Long Key to justify a full day's paddle. But with one of the few public campgrounds on the keys—and one of the most attractive—you might want to consider a stay of two days or more.

INFORMATION: Long Key State Recreation Area, P.O. Box 776, Long Key, FL 33001; 305/664-4815; www.dep.state.fl.us/parks/south /long.html. The SRA is open daily from 8 am to sundown. Entrance fees begin at $3.75 for one person. Rest rooms, water, and a pay phone are all at the site. You can pick up a map of the canoe trail and park at the entrance station.

MAPS: NOAA 11449; USGS Long Key.

HAZARDS: Outside the protected waters that the canoe trail follows boat traffic is common. Tidal range: 1.25 feet.

BASE CAMP: The SRA features one of the few public campgrounds on the keys. 60 car- and kayak-accessible sites are lined up along the ocean side of Long Key. The sites cost $17/night and the campground is open year round. Reservations are recommended, as the sites go fast in this popular park. For a listing of nearby hotel and resort accommodations contact the Islamorada Chamber of Commerce (800/322-5397).

PUT-IN: The entrance to the SRA is on the ocean side of US-1 at MM 67.5. The start of the canoe trail is on the L just past the entrance. Boats can also be launched from the individual campsites.

TAKE-OUT: Same as the put-in or in the campground if you're staying there.

DAY TRIP: *Mangrove Key and Tidal Creek. A 7- or 12-mile paddle that follows a marked trail before heading out onto the open waters of Long Key Bight and the Atlantic Ocean. Difficulty rating: 2.*

Put in at the start of the canoe trail and follow its winding route through mangrove hammocks. At marker #13 (at about 0.75 mile), leave the trail and turn R into Zane Grey Creek. Paddle out to the mouth of the creek at Long Key Bight, a quarter-mile away. Turn R and follow the curve of land as it bends around for just over a mile to the entrance to the bight. Turn SE and then SW and continue to follow the shoreline to Long Key Point, 1.25 miles away. Turn W and paddle along the shore almost 2 miles to an inlet next to an observation tower and a lagoon. From here you have a choice: If you're camping, continue along the shoreline another 1–2 miles to the campground. Otherwise, turn around and retrace your route back to marker #13 on the canoe trail. From there complete the last half-mile of the trail and end back at the put-in.

Bahia Honda State Recreation Area
Atlantic Ocean ◊ Florida Bay

Find any list of the best beaches in the United States, and, inevitably, Bahia Honda will be on it. The small island is rimmed on all sides by wide, sandy beaches shaded by scattered palm trees in a scene that approximates notions of a tropical idyll. The waters just beyond the sand conceal marine habitats that create a painterly effect of light and dark on the water's surface. Sandy-bottomed shallows appear as yellow; broad sea grass beds absorb the sun's light and make the water seem inky black; and coral reefs reflect back an aqua blue, mirroring the unbroken horizon and sky above. Swimming, snorkeling, and scuba diving are all favorite activities at the 600-acre park, which covers all Bahia Honda Key.

Behind the broad band of beach, hammocks of mangrove, silver palm, and satinwood trees cover much of the small island's upland area. A tidal lagoon spreads across the eastern half of the island, divided by the asphalt ribbon of US-1. Among the wildlife that inhabits the park, avian species are most visible: brown pelicans, cormorants, herons, egrets, gulls, and terns are all common residents or visitors. Park facilities include a nature trail, 80-site campground, rental cabins, marina, boat ramps, and a large visitor center with dive shop.

Although for the majority of visitors the beaches are the main attraction at Bahia Honda, most paddlers will want to capitalize on the opportunity to observe the colorful underwater realm on the key's Atlantic side. The reefs here include sponges, soft coral, and small coral heads that harbor spiny lobster, stone crabs, and tropical fish. If conditions are calm, you can spy much of this vivid world from your kayak as you paddle over the reefs. Better yet, anchor your boat in the shallows (not over the reefs) or leave it on shore and spend some time exploring the marine world with snorkeling gear. The proximity of the reefs to shore offers a rare opportunity in the keys to be able to do this without first paddling miles offshore.

At some point on your paddle around the island, you'll

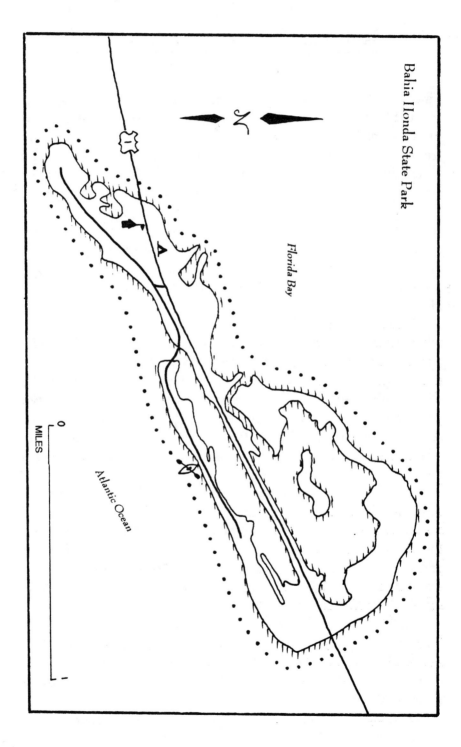

Bahia Honda State Park

Florida Bay

Atlantic Ocean

MILES

0

1

probably want to get out and spend some time swimming or just sunning on the beach. The widest beaches are on the island's Atlantic side, while the Florida Bay side is preferred for swimming. Avoid swimming near Bahia Honda Channel, where the water is deep and the currents swift. Although the beaches of Bahia Honda are probably the most popular in the keys, a kayak will help you find an isolated spot and let you explore the fascinating marine world just beyond the beaches.

INFORMATION: Bahia Honda State Recreation Area; www.dep. state.fl.us/parks/south/bahia.html. The entrance fee is $2.50. A full complement of services is available, including a snack shop and gift shop.

MAPS: NOAA 11445, USGS Big Pine Key, Sevenmile Bridge.

HAZARDS: The currents in Bahia Honda Channel can be very strong. Small pleasure boats ferrying divers and snorkelers are a presence offshore. As you paddle the shallows be sure to keep an eye out for the divers and snorkelers as well. Tidal range: 1.25 feet.

BASE CAMP: The park features a fully developed campground, the westernmost one on the keys. Sites cost $19/night and the campground is open all year. Reservations are highly recommended, especially during peak season in winter. For listings of other nearby accommodations, contact the Marathon Chamber of Commerce (800/262-7284) or the Lower Keys Chamber of Commerce (800/872-3722).

PUT-IN: The entrance to the SRA is at MM 36.8 on US-1. You can put in at the marina boat ramp, but it's just as easy to use the beach access at the 2 parking areas.

TAKE-OUT: Same as the put-in.

DAY TRIP: *Bahia Honda Circuit. Highlights of this 6-mile loop include beautiful beaches, coral reefs and sea grass beds, and mangrove hammocks. Difficulty rating: 3.*

Put in at the first oceanside parking area, where you'll have to carry your kayak down a short flight of steps and across a narrow beach. Paddle E along the beach. Just offshore are the reefs worthy of exploration with snorkeling gear. Unlike at Pennekamp State Park, you can anchor your kayak in waist-high water here and get out and back in with relative ease. Another option is to simply leave it on the beach and wade the short distance to the reefs. Paddle 1 mile to the E end of the island. Turn L and paddle through the channel 1 mile to the Florida Bay side of the island. Follow the shoreline as it curves around past the marina to the larger Bahia Honda Channel, 2 miles away. Paddle through the channel and back around to the Atlantic side of the island. From here, it's just over a mile back to the starting point.

Florida Keys National Wildlife Refuges
Florida Bay

Three adjacent, and, in some places overlapping, national wildlife refuges—Key Deer, Great White Heron, and Key West—encompass a vast area of more than 600 square miles in a rectangular region that extends north and west from the lower keys. Referred to collectively as "the Backcountry," this vast, uninhabited region is accessible only by boat and is open only during daylight hours. While for kayakers, whose range is just a little over twenty miles per day, this means that only a small percentage of the area can be explored per trip, it also ensures that the fragile habitats remain protected from the intense human pressures of the Lower Keys' tourist industry.

Most visits to this region, and the trip described below, begin at the National Key Deer Refuge. The refuge was established in 1957 to protect the diminutive relatives of the white-tailed deer, which had been hunted and crowded almost to extinction by the 1940s. Found nowhere in the world outside of the lower Florida keys, key deer measure just over two feet at the shoulder when they're fully grown. As rare as they are cute, there are only approximately 400 of the animals currently inhabiting Big Pine Key and a handful of surrounding smaller islands. Although habitat loss and a limited range are still concerns, today the gravest threat to the animals comes from motor vehicles, which kill dozens of the deer each year as they graze beside roadways at dawn and dusk. Your best chance of spotting them is on the side of the road to the boat ramp, or along one of several wildlife trails.

Away from the pinelands and fresh-water impoundments of Big Pine Key, the backcountry is characterized by vast stretches of aqua blue waters and dozens of small coral and mangrove keys. This is a region of big sky and endless horizons punctuated only now and then by the rising form of a small green island. A kayak is the ideal vessel for exploring these shallow waters. Marine species such as porpoises and rays are frequently seen, and a kayak's natural stealth will also allow you to observe the hundreds of avian species encountered wading in the flats,

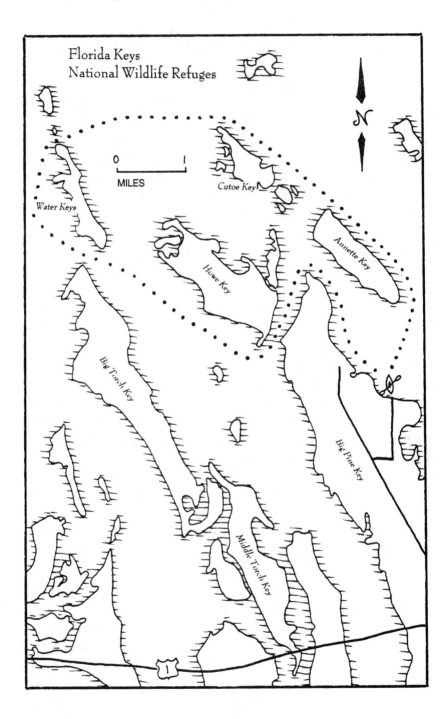

Florida Keys
National Wildlife Refuges

MILES

0   1

Water Keys

Cutoe Key

Howe Key

Annette Key

Big Torch Key

Big Pine Key

Middle Torch Key

N

perched on mangrove limbs, diving for fish, or soaring over head. Egrets, herons, ibis, and roseate spoonbills are just some of the bird varieties common to the backcountry.

With water depths that range from less than a foot to not much more than five or six feet, a kayak provides access even to areas from which most other boats are excluded. Even in a kayak, however, you'll find the going slow in many places, so be sure to allow yourself plenty of time to complete your scheduled route. The trip described below is just one of many routes that you can paddle among the dozen islands within five miles of the launch on Big Pine Key. For information about other boat ramps and exploring other parts of the refuges, inquire at the main refuge office on Key Deer Blvd.

INFORMATION: Florida Keys National Wildlife Refuges, P.O. Box 430510, Big Pine Key, FL 33043-0510; 305/872-2239; www.gorp.com/gorp/resource/us.nwr/fl_natio.htm. The refuge office is located in the large shopping center off Key Deer Blvd. Inside you can pick up refuge maps and brochures. The refuge is open during daylight hours only.

MAPS: NOAA 11445, USGS Big Pine Key, Summerland Key, Horseshoe Keys, Content Keys.

HAZARDS: The refuge's backcountry is relatively remote. Other boaters are usually present in the area, but not usually in the large numbers encountered elsewhere in the keys. Tidal range: 1.25 feet.

BASE CAMP: Camping is not permitted on any of the keys within the refuge. The nearest public campground is at Bahia Honda SP (see separate entry above). Information about hotel, resort, and other accommodations is available from the Lower Keys Chamber of Commerce (800/872-3722) or the Key West Chamber of Commerce (800/648-6269).

PUT-IN: From MM 30.4 on US-1 turn N onto Key Deer Blvd. Go 2.9 miles and turn R onto Big Pine St. Go 0.3 miles and turn L onto

Koehn Ave. Go 0.9 miles to the end of the road and boat ramp.

TAKE-OUT: Same as the put-in.

DAY TRIP: *Backcountry Keys Exploration. This 14-mile route meanders through the backcountry keys to the north and west of Big Pine Key. With a nautical chart the route can easily be shortened or altered to suit your own plans. Difficulty rating: 3.*

From the put-in paddle N 1.5 miles to Annette Key. On the far side of the island, turn NW and paddle beside the mangrove key for 1.5 miles to its other end. Continue in a NWerly direction. In less than 0.5 mile you pass a cluster of small keys and then the larger Cutoe Key. Paddle 1.5 miles to the end of the island. Turn L and head due W toward the N end of Water Keys, 2 miles away. As you pass around the key turn S and follow the island for 1.5 miles to the channel that separates it from the very large Big Torch Key. Turn SE and paddle through the channel and 1 mile to Howe Key. Continue in the same direction for another 2 miles to the W end of Big Pine Key. Turn N and paddle through the channel that separates the two keys. At the N tip of Big Pine Key, just over 1 mile away, turn S and follow the line of the island 2 miles back to the put-in on Koehn Ave.

Key West
Atlantic Ocean ◊ Florida Bay

Key West is a tough sell in a guide to sea kayaking. In truth, the town is best seen on foot, where its narrow shaded lanes and rich architectural and cultural heritage can be most fully appreciated. And the waters that surround it are often jam packed with all kinds of watercraft, from commercial fishing vessels to cigarette boats to whining jet-skis. It's included here because Key West is the heart and soul of the keys, and one of those quintessential American places that just shouldn't be passed by. In other words, if you come to the lower keys, you'd be a fool not to visit Key West. And if you use the town as a base for explorations further afield, you can not only wander its charming streets, but you might be tempted to paddle the waters that surround it and offer an entirely different perspective of the city. It is, after all, an island, one that's perfectly sized for a day's circumnavigation.

Ponce de Leon was the first European to set sight on what is now Key West. A century after his visit it was showing up on maps as *Cayo Hueso*, Spanish for Bone Key, an homage, apparently, to the dead men's bones that lay scattered on the island. Highlights of the island's history over the next three centuries include unchecked pirate attacks, a steady shipwreck and salvage business created by the offshore reefs, a boom-and-bust cigar-manufacturing business that reinforced the city's link to Cuba, Henry Flagler's ill-fated railroad that briefly connected Key West to the Florida mainland, an infamous—and extremely profitable—traffic in rumrunning during Prohibition, and finally, its current role as a tourist destination and haven for artists, writers, and others drawn by the lazy, *laissez faire* attitude of the subtropical, end-of-the-line city.

As you circle the island, you pass the precincts and landmarks that attest to the rich, colorful history of America's southernmost city. On the island's northwest corner sits Mallory Square, the most popular gathering place for the daily ritual of saluting the setting sun as it slips beneath the blue-green waters of the Gulf of Mexico. The waterfront cluster of warehouses and docks dates

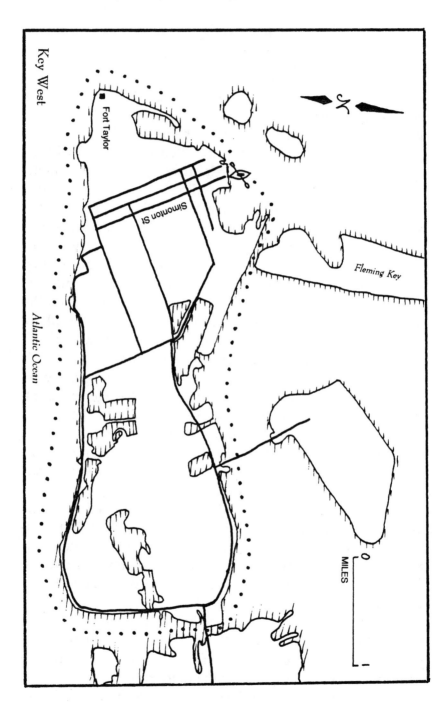

back to the city's earliest days and the historic district fans out to the south and east. Just south of the square is the Truman Annex, the building dubbed The Little White House because the former president spent so many working vacations here. Not far away at the island's southwest corner is Fort Zachary Taylor. Construction on the fort, which took 21 years to complete, was begun in 1845 when Key West was Florida's largest city. Today the trapezoidal fort is listed on the National Register of Historic Places. It anchors a park that includes the best beach in Key West. Paddlers can land here for a lunch break or explore the fort and grounds.

On the island's eastern half buildings of historical note give way to hotels, commercial strips, and long beaches that front the reef-calmed waters of the Atlantic Ocean. The public beaches on this side of the island make it most popular with all sorts of watersports enthusiasts: jet-skiers, windsurfers, parasailers, and just regular sailors are all abundant. A sea kayaker seeking pristine waters and quiet isolation will have to look elsewhere.

INFORMATION: Key West Chamber of Commerce, 402 Wall St., Key West, FL 33040; 800/648-6269. You can pick up a map of the town at the Chamber office downtown. Paddling supplies are available at a couple of outfitters in Key West.

MAPS: NOAA 11441; USGS Key West, Boca Chica Key.

HAZARDS: Boat traffic here is heavier than anywhere else in the keys. You'll encounter power boats and jet skis on both the ocean and bay sides, and wind surfers on the ocean side. You may want to time your paddle for a weekday or the off-season. The currents on the island's W edge, where the Gulf and Ocean collide, can get quite rough. Tidal range: 1.5 feet.

BASE CAMP: There's no public campground near Key West (the closest is 35 miles east at Bahia Honda SP) and camping is not allowed on any of the backcountry keys. Hotel, motel, and B&B accommodations, however, are abundant. Contact the Chamber of Commerce for listings.

PUT-IN: A boat ramp and small, sandy landing are located at the N end of Simonton St in downtown Key West.

TAKE-OUT: Same as the put-in.

DAY TRIP: *Key West Circuit. This 13-mile trip circles the island of Key West, passing the downtown district, a historic fort, and several beaches. One drawback to consider is the boat traffic, which can be considerable, especially on weekends. Difficulty rating: 4.*

Put in at the sandy landing next to the boat ramp at the end of Simonton St. Paddle out into the harbor and follow the curve of the island around to the W and then S. Almost immediately you're paddling past the downtown waterfront, with restaurants, shops, hotels, and boat slips all in view. The boat traffic is heaviest in this area, so be sure to exercise caution. Follow the W end of Key West S to Fort Taylor. If you like, you can land on the beach here and get out and explore the grounds. Paddlers not wanting to cover the entire 13-mile trip around the island can use this as a convenient turning around point. When you reach the fort, turn E and follow the S end of the island for 4 miles, passing vacation homes, hotels, and a couple of public beaches along the way. The beaches provide another chance to come ashore for a while and maybe grab a bite to eat. At the E end of Key West, turn N and enter Cow Key Channel, with Cow Key and Stock Island on the R. The busy boating channel runs for almost 4 miles to the N end of Key West. When you get there, turn W and paddle just over 3 miles, perhaps into one of those famed Key West sunsets, until you reach the boat ramp.

Outfitters & Guides

The following businesses sell and rent sea kayaks and related equipment and/or offer guided trips. They are arranged geographically, from north to south, in a manner that very roughly corresponds to the layout of the main part of this book. We hope this makes finding a place to buy or rent a sea kayak as easy as possible. These businesses are included here as a service to our readers; the author and Out There Press have not received compensation from any of them.

Georgia

Roswell
Go With the Flow Sports—4 Elizabeth Way; 770/992-3200
Open M–F: 10–7
Sales & Rentals

Atlanta
High Country—3906 Roswell Rd; 404/814-0999
Open M–Sa: 9–9; Su: 12–6
Sales & Rentals

REI—1165 Perimeter West #200; 770/901-9200
Open M–F: 10–9; Sa: 10–7; Su: 11–6
Sales

REI—1800 Northeast Expressway NE; 404/633-6508
Open M–F: 10–9; Sa: 10–7; Su: 11–6
Sales

Columbus
Outdoor World—3201 Macon Rd; 706/563-2113
Open M–F: 10–8; Sa: 10–6
Sales

Savannah
Wilderness Outfitters Inc—103 East Montgomery Cross Rd
912/927-2071. Open M–W, Sa: 10–6; Th–F: 10–8; Su: 1–6
Sales

Tybee Island
Sea Kayak Georgia—1101 2nd Ave; 912/786-8732
Open Su-Sa: 8–8
Sales, Rentals, & Guided Tours

St Simons Island
Southeast Adventure Outfitters—313 Mallory St; 912/638-6732
Open daily: 10–6
Sales, Rentals, & Guided Tours

Brunswick
Southeast Adventure Outfitters—1200 Glynn Ave; 912/265-5292
Open daily: 10–6
Sales, Rentals, & Guided Tours

St Marys
Southeast Adventure Outfitters—104 B St Marys Rd
912/876-8481. Open daily: 8–6
Sales, Rentals, & Guided Tours

Florida

Pensacola
Old Sarge's Outdoor South—1102 North 9th Ave; 850/433-1619
Open M–Sa: 9–6
Sales

Milton
Adventures Unlimited Canoe—8974 Tomahawk Landing Rd;
850/623-6197. Open Su–Th: 8–4; F–Sa: 8–5
Sales & Rentals

Panama City
Canoe Shop—1129 Beck Ave; 850/763-2311
Open Tu–F: 10–6; Sa: 8–6
Sales, Rentals, & Guided Tours

Niceville
Splashdance Windsurfing—207 Government Ave; 850/678-1637
Open M–Sa: 9–5
Sales, Rentals, & Guided Tours

Tallahassee
Canoe Shop—1115 W Orange Ave; 904/576-5335
Open M–F: 10–6; Sa–Su: 8–6
Sales, Rentals,& Guided Tours

Jacksonville
Black Creek Trading Post—10051 Skinner Lake Dr; 904/645-7003
Open M–F: 10–8; Sa: 10–6; Su: 12–5
Sales, Rentals, & Guided Tours

Outdoor Adventures—1625 Emerson St; 904/393-9030
Open M–F: 9–5
Rentals & Guided Tours

Neptune Beach
Aqua East Surf Shop—696 Atlantic Blvd; 904/246-2550
Open M–Sa: 9–9; Su: 9–6
Sales & Rentals

Ponte Vedra Beach
Blue Water Kayaks—226-5 Solano Rd #136; 904/280-9320
Open by appointment
Guided Tours

Orange Park
Black Creek Trading Post—410 Blanding Blvd; 904/272-6996
Open M–F: 10–8; Sa: 10–6; Su: 12–5
Sales, Rentals, & Guided Tours

High Springs
Silent Waters—15 Northeast 2nd Ave; 904/454-1991
Open M–Sa: 10–6; Su: 12–5
Sales & Guided Tours

St. Augustine
Coastal Kayak Company—4255 A1A South; 904/471-4144
Open by appointment
Sales, Rentals, & Guided Tours

Whole Earth Outfitters—835 Anastasia Blvd; 904/824-6161
Open M–F: 9–5:30, Su–Sa: 9–4
Sales & Guided Tours

Gainesville
Brasington's Trail Shop Inc—2331 Northwest 13th St
352/372-0521. Open M–W: 10–6; Th: 10–8; F–Sa: 10–6; Su: 1–5
Sales& Guided Tours

New Smyrna Beach
Island Rentals—3502 South Atlantic Ave; 904/428-0068
Open daily: 10–8 (winter), 8:30–10:30 (summer)
Sales & Rentals

Cedar Key
Cedar Key Kayak—3rd St; 352/543-9437
Open daily: Daylight hours
Rentals

Umatilla
Eustis Outdoor Shop—37826 State Rd 19; 352/669-1224
Open Tu–Sa: 9:30–6
Sales

Homosassa
Homosassa Kayak & Expedition Co—5300 S Cherokee Way
352/628-3183; Open W–Su: 9–5
Sales, Rentals, & Guided Trips

Altamonte Springs
Travel Country—1101 East Highway 436; 407/831-0777
Open M–F: 10–8; Sa:10–6, Su: 12–5
Sales & Guided Trips

Cocoa Beach
Banana River Kayaks—165 North Orlando Ave; 407/784-3235
Open by appointment
Guided Tours

Satellite Beach
Extreme's Sports—294 East Eau Gallie Blvd; 407/779-4228
Open M–Sa: 10–6; Su: 12–6
Sales, Rentals, & Guided Tours

Auburndale
Action Watersports—235 East Lake Ave; 941/957-4148
Open M–F: 9–4, Sa:9–12
Sales & Guided Trips

Thonotosassa
Canoe Escape Inc—9335 Fowler Ave; 813/986-2067
Open M–F: 9–5; Sa–Su: 8–6
Sales

Clearwater
Agua Azul—17952 US Hwy 19 N; 813/530-7555
Open Tu–F: 10–6; Sa: 10–5; Su: 12–4
Sales

Largo
Suncoast Sea Kayaks Inc—10900 Oakhurst Rd; 813/595-3220
Open Tu–F: 10–5:30; Sa: 10–4
Sales

St Petersburg
Canoes Country Outfitters—6493 54th Ave N; 813/545-4554
Open M–F: 9–7; Sa: 9–5
Sales & Rentals

Holmes Beach
Florida Sports—5501 Marina Dr; 941/778-5883
Open Tu–Sa: 9–5; Su 12–4
Sales, Rentals, & Guided Trips

Vero Beach
Adventure Kayaking—3435 Aviation Blvd; 561/567-0522
Open M–Sa: 9–5
Sales, Rentals, & Guided Trips

Sarasota
Silent Sports of Florida—7660 Tamiami Trail
941/922-4042. Open daily: 9–4:30
Rentals & Guided Tours

Sweetwater Kayaks—5263 Ocean Blvd; 941/346-1179
Open M–Sa: 10–6
Sales, Rentals, & Guided Tours

Stuart
Cove Kayak Center Inc—4595 SE Dixie Hwy; 561/220-4079
Open by appointment
Rentals & Guided Trips

Jupiter

Canoe Outfitters of Florida—9060 West Indiantown Rd
561/746-7053. Open W–Su: 8–5
Sales & Rentals

Southern Exposure Sea Kayaks—18487 Southeast Federal Hwy;
561/575-4530. Open by appointment
Guided Tours

North Palm Beach

Adventure Times Kayaking—521 Northlake Blvd; 561/881-7218
Open Tu–F: 10–6; Sa: 9–5; Su: 11-4
Sales, Rentals, & Guided Trips

West Palm Beach

Outdoor Sports World—3415 South Dixie Hwy; 561/833-7539
Open M–Sa: 9–6
Sales

Sanibel

Wildside Adventures—15041 Captiva Dr; 941/395-2925
Open daily: 9–7
Sales, Rentals, & Guided Tours

Pompano Beach

Atlantic Coast Kayak Company—1869 South Dixie Hwy;
954/781-0073. Open Tu–F: 10–6; Sa: 10–5
Sales, Rentals, & Guided Tours

Marco Island

Get Wet Sports—240 Royal Palm Dr; 941/394-9557
Open daily: 10–6
Sales, Rentals, & Guided Tours

Hollywood

Waterways Kayak & Outfitters—1406 North Ocean Dr
954/921-8944. Open M–F: 12–6; Sa–Su: 9–6
Sales, Rentals, & Guided Tours

Dania
Obsession Water Sports—222 North Federal Hwy; 954/921-5802
Open M–Sa: 10–7; Su: 10–6
Sales

Miami
Jet's Florida Outfitters—9696 Bird Rd; 305/221-1371
Open M–Sa: 9–9; Su :10–6
Sales

Urban Trails Kayak Rentals—10800 Collins Ave; 305/860-0888
Open daily: 9–7
Sales, Rentals, & Guided Tours

Waterplay—2550 South Bayshore Dr; 305/860-0888
Open M–Sa: 10–7; Su :12–4
Sales

Key Largo
Florida Bay Outfitters—104050 Overseas Hwy; 305/451-3018
Open daily: 9–6
Sales, Rentals, & Guided Tours

Marathon
Ocean Paddler—50 Coco Plum Dr; 305/743-0131
Open by appointment
Guided Tours

World Class Angler—5050 Overseas Hwy; 305/743-6139
Open daily: 7–6
Rentals

Islamorada
Kayaking Florida—84,000 Overseas Hwy; 305/664-9494
Open daily: 9–6
Sales, Rentals, & Guided Trips

Big Pine Key
Lost World Adventures—Overseas Hwy, MM 30; 305/872-8950.
Open by appointment
Rentals and Guided Tours

Reflections Kayak Nature Tours—Parmer's Place Resort Hotel;
305/872-2896/-2157. Open by appointment
Guided Tours

Key West
CAYO Carbie Kayak Rental—1018 Truman Ave; 305/296-4115
Open M–Sa: 10:30–6:30; Su 11–4
Rentals & Guided Tours

Mosquito Coast Island Outfitters—1107 Duval St; 305/294-7178
Open Su-Sa: 10–11
Guided Tours

Index

Order Form

Return to:
Out There Press
P.O. Box 1173
Asheville, NC 28802

Name: _____

Address: _____

City/State/Zip: _____

QTY	Guides to Backcountry Travel & Adventure	Price	Total
	North Carolina	$16	
	Virginia	$16	
	South Carolina	$15	
	West Virginia	$15	
	Other Titles		
	Sea Kayaking Florida...	$15	
	Sea Kayaking the Carolinas	$15	
	NC Residents add 6% sales tax		
	Shipping		$3
	Order Total		

Please enclose a check or money order for the total amount and return to the above address. Allow 2 weeks for delivery.

Field Notes

Field Notes

Field Notes

Field Notes